The Reading Teacher's Book of Lists

Edward Bernard Fry, Ph.D.

Jacqueline K. Polk, M.A.

Dona Fountoukidis, Ed.D.

Prentice-Hall, Inc.   Englewood Cliffs, NJ

Prentice-Hall International, Inc., *London*
Prentice-Hall of Australia, Pty. Ltd., *Sydney*
Prentice-Hall Canada, Inc., *Toronto*
Prentice-Hall of India Private Ltd., *New Delhi*
Prentice-Hall of Japan, Inc., *Tokyo*
Prentice-Hall of Southeast Asia Pte. Ltd., *Singapore*
Whitehall Books, Ltd., *Wellington, New Zealand*
Editora Prentice-Hall do Brasil, Ltda., *Rio de Janeiro*

Library of Congress Cataloging in Publication Data

Fry, Edward Bernard
   The reading teacher's book of lists.
   1. Reading—Miscellanea. 2. Curriculum planning—
Miscellanea. 3. Tutors and tutoring—Miscellanea.
4. Handbooks, vade-mecums, etc. I. Polk, Jacqueline K.
II. Fountoukidis, Dona. III. Title. IV. Title: Book of
lists.
LB1050.2.F79 1984   428.4'07   83-21201

ISBN 0-13-762112-4

Printed in the United States of America

ABOUT THE AUTHORS

Edward Bernard Fry, Ph.D., is Director of the Reading Center and Professor of Education at Rutgers University in New Brunswick, New Jersey. Dr. Fry teaches courses for graduate and undergraduate students and serves on dissertation committees. As the Reading Center director, he provides instruction for children with reading problems, conducts statewide reading conferences, and provides reading improvement courses for college students and teacher-training reading courses for undergraduates.

Dr. Fry has authored a number of practical guides for reading teachers, including *Elementary Reading Instruction* (McGraw-Hill, 1977), *Reading for Classroom and Clinic* (McGraw-Hill, 1972), *Teaching Faster Reading* (Cambridge University Press, 1963), and *The Emergency Reading Teacher's Manual* (Dreier, 1969). He also has developed a variety of curriculum materials, including typing courses for children, filmstrips, overhead transparencies, card reader programs on phonics and basic vocabulary, reading improvement drill books, criterion-referenced tests, and videotape reading improvement programs for industries and universities.

Jacqueline K. Polk, M.A., has had a wide range of teaching experiences in reading. She has served as a classroom teacher, a remedial reading specialist, and a reading coordinator at the elementary school level; has taught developmental reading and study skills at the college level; and has trained reading teachers. Ms. Polk also has conducted numerous workshops for teachers in decoding, comprehension, grammar, and gifted education, and she has developed curricula at the elementary and high school levels in reading and other content areas in gifted education. She soon will complete her doctoral degree in reading at Rutgers University.

Dona Fountoukidis, Ed.D., has held a variety of teaching positions. In Japan she taught English to Japanese junior and senior high school students. In the United States she has taught, primarily at the college level, courses ranging from basic reading and writing to teacher training in areas such as content area reading and educational psychology. Dr. Fountoukidis currently is affiliated with the Reading Disabilities Research Institute of Rutgers University and Rutgers Medical School, where she is engaged in research concerned with the development of word identification skills in children.

PREFACE

This book has one main idea—to provide useful and occasionally amusing information for teachers of reading.

However, it is a "nonbook" in that it does not have a beginning, a conclusion, or a plot. It basically has very little prose and consists primarily of lists of words, phonetic elements, meanings, symbols, and miscellaneous ideas.

This book provides, under one cover, diverse types of information needed in developing reading lessons, preparing curriculum materials, and tutoring. The level of material ranges from beginning readers in elementary schools, through developmental materials for secondary schools.

The nonlist content of the book is composed primarily of information for teachers, such as teaching suggestions, testing tips and terms, and some ideas tinged with a bit of humor.

So, make your way through this nonbook and get acquainted with it. Glance at the table of contents if you want an overview, or just open to the middle and start browsing. You can start from the back and go forward or from the front and move toward the back. On another day you can start in the middle and move either way. This book is nonlinear. But that doesn't mean it's not organized; the structure can be seen in the table of contents or in the headings on each page.

We have made a few teaching suggestions for most lists, but this is basically an information source. It challenges you to be creative and gives you the raw information to be creative with.

We think we have provided the largest list of phonograms anywhere, the most useful list of high-frequency words, and a whole lot more; but we will let you be the final judge of the value of this material. Without bragging or complaining too much, we will tell you that it was a lot harder to develop, gather, edit, and organize this material than we ever anticipated. We hope our efforts pay off in your classroom. We would also be pleased to receive additional suggestions from you.

Edward Fry
Jacqueline Polk
Dona Fountoukidis

Contents

I
WORDS

LOOK ALIKES, SOUND ALIKES, AND NEAR MISSES

Words that sound alike but are spelled differently (homophones), words that look alike but are pronounced differently (homographs), and words that are near misses (e.g., *accept* and *except*) can cause lots of confusion.

These words have troubled generations of spellers, have harassed poor readers, and are the positive curse of students of English as a second language (ESL). Incorrect use of these words in oral and written communication can be the mark of a poorly educated person.

Students of all ages enjoy learning, discovering, and playing with these words. For teachers, they provide interesting lessons, a chance for clever and intelligent explanations, and a great way to expand student vocabularies.

Here are a few teaching suggestions:

1. Teach one or two pairs each day, and at the end of the week use them in either a spelling lesson or a word meaning drill.

2. Put a homophone or homograph pair on the board and ask students to come up with others; let the list build for two weeks.

3. Develop some tricky sentences, such as "I will _____ you at the _____ market." Students fill in *meet* and *meat*. Have classes engage in competition: send two sentences next door and see if the next class can figure them out. The second class can respond with two more sentences.

4. Divide the class into two teams. You provide a homograph and one meaning. Each team takes turn trying to come up with another meaning. If one team can't do it within a given time limit, the other team gets to try.

The following is not the longest possible list of homophones. We have intentionally omitted some that use rare and very difficult words. However, it is pretty extensive, and certainly every teacher needs a good list of homophones in his or her bag of tricks.

Homophones—Words That Sound the Same

ads (advertisements)	air (oxygen)	all (everything)
adz (axlike tool)	heir (successor)	awl (tool)
	aisle (path)	
ail (be sick)	I'll (I will)	allowed (permitted)
ale (beverage)	isle (island)	aloud (audible)

altar (as in a church)
alter (change)

arc (part of a circle)
ark (boat)

ate (did eat)
eight (number)

aural (by ear)
oral (by mouth)

awful (terrible)
offal (entrails)

aye (yes)
eye (organ of sight)

bail (throw water out)
bale (bundle)

band (plays music)
banned (forbidden)

bard (poet)
barred (having bars)

bare (nude)
bear (animal)

base (foundation)
bass (deep tone)

be (exist)
bee (insect)

beach (shore)
beech (tree)

beat (whip)
beet (vegetable)

beau (boyfriend)
bow (decorative knot)

bell (something you ring)
belle (pretty woman)

berry (fruit)
bury (put underground)

berth (bunk)
birth (being born)

bight (slack part of rope)
bite (chew)

boar (hog)
bore (drill a hole)

board (lumber)
bored (uninterested)

boll (cotton pod)
bowl (dish; game)

born (delivered at birth)
borne (carried)

borough (town)
burrow (dig)

bough (of a tree)
bow (of a ship)

boy (male child)
bouy (floating object)

brake (stop)
break (smash)

bread (food)
bred (cultivated)

brewed (steeped)
brood (flock)

brews (steeps)
bruise (bump)

but (except)
butt (end)

buy (purchase)
by (near)
bye (farewell)

cache (hiding place)
cash (money)

canvas (cloth)
canvass (survey)

capital (money; city)
capitol (building)

carat (weight of metal)
caret (proofreader's mark)
carrot (vegetable)

cast (throw; actors in a
    play)
caste (social class)

cell (prison room)
sell (exchange for money)

cellar (basement)
seller (one who sells)

censor (ban)
sensor (detection device)

cent (penny)
scent (odor)
sent (did send)

chalk (writing
    instrument)

chock (wedge under a
    wheel)

cheap (inexpensive)
cheep (bird call)

chews (bites)
choose (select)

chord (musical notes)
cord (string)

climb (ascend)
clime (climate)

close (shut)
clothes (clothing)

coal (fuel)
cole (cabbage)

coarse (rough)
course (path; school
    subject)

colonel (military rank)
kernel (grain of corn)

complement (complete set)
compliment (good word)

coop (chicken pen)
coupe (car)

core (center)
corps (army group)

council (legislative body)
counsel (advise)

creak (grating noise)
creek (stream)

crews (groups of workers)
cruise (sail)

dam (barrier)
damn (curse)

dear (precious)
deer (animal)

days (plural of *day*)
daze (stun)

dew (mist)
do (act)
due (payable now)

die (expire)
dye (color)

dine (eat)
dyne (unit of force)

doe (female deer)
dough (bread mixture)

done (finished)
dun (gray)

ewe (female sheep)
yew (shrub)
you (personal pronoun)

faint (weak)
feint (pretend attack)

fair (honest)
fare (cost of transportation)

feat (accomplishment)
feet (plural of *foot*)

find (discover)
fined (charged money as penalty)

fir (tree)
fur (animal covering)

flair (talent)
flare (flaming signal)

flea (insect)
flee (run away)

flew (did fly)
flu (influenza)
flue (shaft)

flour (milled grain)
flower (bloom)

for (in favor of)
fore (front part)
four (number)

forth (forward)
fourth (after third)

foul (bad)
fowl (bird)

gilt (golden)
guilt (opposite of *innocence*)

gnu (antelope)
knew (did know)
new (opposite of *old*)

gorilla (animal)
guerrilla (irregular soldier)

grate (grind)
great (large)

groan (moan)
grown (cultivated)

guessed (surmised)
guest (company)

hail (ice; salute)
hale (healthy)

hair (on head)
hare (rabbit)

hall (passage)
haul (carry)

hangar (storage building)
hanger (to hang things on)

heal (make well)
heel (bottom of foot)

hear (listen)
here (at this place)

heard (listened)
herd (group of animals)

hew (carve)
hue (color)

higher (above)
hire (employ)

him (male pronoun)
hymn (religious song)

hoarse (husky voice)
horse (animal)

hole (opening)
whole (complete)

hour (60 minutes)
our (possessive pronoun)

idle (lazy)
idol (god)

in (opposite of *out*)
inn (hotel)

its (possessive pronoun)
it's (it is)

jam (fruit jelly)
jamb (window part)

knight (military servant)
night (evening)

knit (weave with yarn)
nit (louse egg)

knot (tangle)
not (in no manner)

lead (metal)
led (guided)

leak (crack)
leek (vegetable)

lessen (make less)
lesson (instruction)

lie (falsehood)
lye (alkaline solution)

lieu (instead of)
Lou (name)

load (burden)
lode (vein of ore)

loan (something
    borrowed)
lone (single)

loot (steal)
lute (musical instrument)

made (manufactured)
maid (servant)

mail (send by post)
male (masculine)

main (most important)
Maine (state)
mane (hair)

mall (courtyard)
maul (attack)

mantel (over a fireplace)
mantle (cloak)

massed (grouped)
mast (support)

meat (beef)
meet (greet)

miner (coal digger)
minor (juvenile)

missed (failed to attain)
mist (fog)

moan (groan)
mown (cut down)

mode (fashion)
mowed (cut down)

morn (morning)
mourn (grieve)

muscle (flesh)
mussel (shellfish)

nay (no)
neigh (whinny)

none (not any)
nun (religious sister)

oh (exclamation)
owe (be indebted)

one (number)
won (triumphed)

or (conjunction)
ore (mineral deposit)

pail (bucket)
pale (white)

pain (discomfort)
pane (window glass)

pair (two of a kind)
pare (peel)

passed (went by)
past (former)

peace (tranquility)
piece (part)

peak (mountaintop)
peek (look)

peal (ring)
peel (pare)

peer (equal)
pier (dock)

per (for each)
purr (cat sound)

plain (simple)
plane (flat surface)

plum (fruit)
plumb (lead weight)

pole (stick)
poll (vote)

pore (ponder)
pour (flow freely)

pray (worship)
prey (victim)

principal (chief)
principle (rule)

profit (benefit)
prophet (seer)

rain (precipitation)
reign (royal authority)
rein (harness)

raise (put up)
raze (tear down)

rap (hit)
wrap (cover)

read (peruse)
reed (plant)

read (perused)
red (color)

real (genuine)
reel (spool)

rest (relax)
wrest (take from)

right (correct)
rite (ceremony)
write (inscribe)

ring (circular band)
wring (squeeze)

road (street)
rode (was transported)
rowed (used oars)

roe (fish egg)
row (line)

role (character)
roll (turn over; bread)

root (part of a plant)
route (highway)

rose (flower)
rows (lines)

rot (decay)
wrought (formed)

rote (by habit)
wrote (did write)

rude (impolite)
rued (was sorry)

rung (crosspiece)
wrung (squeezed)

rye (grain)
wry (twisted)

sail (travel by boat)
sale (bargain)

scene (setting)
seen (viewed)

sea (ocean)
see (visualize)

seam (joining mark)
seem (appear to be)

sear (singe)
seer (prophet)

sew (mend)
so (in order that)
sow (plant)

shear (cut)
sheer (transparent)

shoe (foot covering)
shoo (drive away)

shone (beamed)
shown (exhibited)

side (flank)
sighed (audible breath)

scull (boat; row)
skull (head)

slay (kill)
sleigh (sled)

slew (killed)
slue (swamp)

soar (fly)
sore (painful)

sole (only)
soul (spirit)

some (portion)
sum (total)

son (male offspring)
sun (star)

staid (proper)
stayed (remained)

stair (step)
stare (look intently)

stake (post)
steak (meat)

stationary (fixed)
stationery (paper)

steal (rob)
steel (metal)

stile (gate)
style (fashion)

straight (not crooked)
strait (channel of water)

suite (connected rooms)
sweet (sugary)

tail (animal's appendage)
tale (story)

tea (drink)
tee (holder for golf ball)

teas (plural of *tea*)
tease (mock)

team (crew)
teem (be full)

tear (cry)
tier (level)

tern (sea bird)
turn (rotate)

their (possessive pronoun)
there (at that place)
they're (they are)

theirs (possessive
    pronoun)
there's (there is)

threw (tossed)
through (finished)

throne (king's seat)
thrown (tossed)

tic (twitch)
tick (insect)

tide (ebb and flow)
tied (bound)

to (toward)
too (also)
two (number)

toad (frog)
towed (pulled)

toe (digit of the foot)
tow (pull)

told (informed)
tolled (rang)

trussed (tied)
trust (confidence)

vain (conceited)
vane (wind indicator)
vein (blood vessel)

vale (valley)
veil (face cover)

vary (change)
very (absolutely)

vice (bad habit)
vise (clamp)

wade (walk in water)
weighed (measured heaviness)

wail (cry)
whale (sea mammal)

waist (middle)
waste (trash)

wait (linger)
weight (heaviness)

waive (forgive)
wave (swell)

ware (pottery)
wear (have on)

way (road)
weigh (measure heaviness)

we (pronoun)
wee (small)

weak (not strong)
week (seven days)

weather (climate)
whether (if)

weave (interlace)
we've (we have)

we'd (we would)
weed (plant)

wet (moist)
whet (sharpen)

which (what one)
witch (sorceress)

who's (who is)
whose (possessive of *who*)

wood (of a tree)
would (is willing to)

yoke (harness)
yolk (egg center)

your (possessive pronoun)
you're (you are)

Homographs—Words That Look the Same

affect (influence)
(pretend)

alight (get down from)
(on fire)

angle (shape formed by two connected lines)
(fish with hook and line)

arch (curved structure)
(chief)

arms (body parts)
(weapons)

august (majestic)

August (eighth month of the year)

axes (plural of *ax*)
(plural of *axis*)

bail (money for release)
(handle of a pail)
(throw water out)

ball (round object)
(formal dance)

band (group of musicians)
(thin strip for binding)

bank (mound)
(place of financial business)
(row of things)
(land along a river)

bark (tree covering)
    (sound a dog makes)
    (sailboat)

base (bottom)
    (morally low)

bass (low male voice)
    (kind of fish)

baste (pour liquid on while roasting)
    (sew with long stitches)

bat (club)
    (flying mammal)
    (wink)

batter (hit repeatedly)
    (liquid mixture used for cakes)
    (baseball player)

bay (part of a sea)
    (aromatic leaf used in cooking)
    (reddish brown)
    (alcove between columns)
    (howl)

bear (large animal)
    (support; carry)

better (one who bets)
    (more desirable)

bill (statement of money owed)
    (beak)

bit (small piece)
    (tool for drilling)
    (did bite)

blaze (fire)
    (mark a trail or a tree)
    (make known)

blow (hard hit)
    (send forth a stream of air)

bluff (steep bank or cliff)
    (fool or mislead)

bob (weight at the end of a line)
    (move up and down)
Bob (nickname for Robert)

boil (bubbling of hot liquid)
    (red swelling on the skin)

boom (deep sound)
    (long beam)
    (sudden increase in size)

boon (benefit)
    (merry)

bore (make a hole)
    (make weary)
    (did bear)

bound (limit)
    (obliged)
    (spring back)
    (on the way)

bow (weapon for shooting arrows)
    (forward part of a ship)
    (bend in greeting or respect)

bowl (rounded dish)
    (play the game of bowling)

box (four-sided container)
    (kind of evergreen shrub)
    (strike with the hand)

bridge (way over an obstacle)
    (card game)

brush (tool for sweeping)
    (bushes)

buck (male deer)
    (slang for *dollar*)

buffer (something that softens)
    (pad for polishing)

buffet (cabinet for dishes and linens)
    (self-serve meal)
    (strike)

"The Reading Teacher's Book of Lists, © 1984 Prentice-Hall, Inc., Englewood Cliffs, NJ 07632. By E. Fry, J. Polk, and D. Fountoukidis."

butt (thicker end of a tool)
    (object of ridicule)

can (able to)
    (metal container)

carp (complain)
    (kind of fish)

case (condition)
    (box or container)

chap (crack or become rough)
    (boy or man)

chop (cut with something sharp)
    (jaw)
    (irregular motion)
    (cut of meat)

chord (two or more musical notes
    together)
    (an emotional response)

chow (breed of dog)
    (slang for *food*)

chuck (throw or toss)
    (cut of beef)

cleave (cut)
    (hold on to)

clip (cut)
    (fasten)

close (shut)
    (near)

clove (fragrant spice)
    (section of a bulb)

cobbler (one who mends shoes)
    (fruit pie with one crust)

cock (rooster)
    (tilt upward)

colon (mark of punctuation)
    (lower part of the large intestine)

commune (talk intimately)
    (group of people living
    together)

compact (firmly packed together)
    (agreement)

compound (having more than one part)
    (enclosed yard)

con (swindle)
    (against)

console (cabinet)
    (ease grief)

content (all things inside)
    (satisfied)

converse (talk)
    (opposite)

corporal (of the body)
    (low-ranking officer)

count (name numbers in order)
    (nobleman)

counter (long table in a store or
    restaurant)
    (one who counts)
    (opposite)

crow (loud cry of a rooster)
    (large black bird)
Crow (tribe of American Indians)

cue (signal)
    (long stick used in a game of pool)

curry (rub and clean a horse)
    (spicy seasoning)

date (day, month, and year)
    (sweet dark fruit)

defer (put off)
    (yield to another)

demean (lower in dignity)
    (humble oneself)

desert (dry barren region)
    (go away from)
    (suitable reward or punishment)

die (stop living)
    (tool)

do (act; perform)
    (first tone on the musical scale)

dock (wharf)
    (cut some off)

does (plural of *doe*)
    (present tense of *to do*)

dove (pigeon)
    (did dive)

down (from a higher to a lower place)
    (soft feathers)
    (grassy land)

dredge (dig up)
    (sprinkle with flour or sugar)

dresser (one who dresses)
    (bureau)

drove (did drive)
    (flock; herd; crowd)

dub (give a title)
    (add voice or music to a film)

duck (large wild bird)
    (lower suddenly)
    (type of cotton cloth)

ear (organ of hearing)
    (part of certain plants)

egg (oval or round body laid by a bird)
    (encourage)

elder (older)
    (small tree)

entrance (going in)
    (delight; charm)

excise (tax)
    (remove)

fair (beautiful; lovely)
    (just; honest)
    (showing of farm goods)
    (bazaar)

fan (device to stir up the air)
    (admirer)

fast (speedy)
    (go without food)

fawn (young deer)
    (try to get favor by slavish acts)

fell (did fall)
    (cut down a tree)
    (deadly)

felt (did feel)
    (type of cloth)

file (drawer; folder)
    (steel tool to smooth rough material)

fine (high quality)
    (money paid as punishment)

firm (solid; hard)
    (business; company)

fit (suitable)
    (sudden attack)

flag (banner)
    (get tired)

flat (smooth)
    (apartment)

fleet (group of ships)
    (rapid)

flight (act of flying)
    (act of fleeing)

flounder (struggle)
    (kind of fish)

fluke (lucky stroke in games)
    (kind of fish)

fly (insect)
(move through the air with wings)

foil (prevent carrying out plans)
(metal sheet)
(long narrow sword)

fold (bend over on itself)
(pen for sheep)

forearm (part of the body)
(prepare for trouble ahead)

forge (blacksmith shop)
(move ahead)

forte (strong point)
(loud)

found (did find)
(set up; establish)

founder (sink)
(one who establishes)

fray (become ragged)
(fight)

fresh (newly made; not stale)
(impudent; bold)

fret (worry)
(ridges on a guitar)

fry (cook in shallow pan)
(young fish)

fuse (slow-burning wick)
(melt together)

gall (bile)
(annoy)

game (pastime)
(lame)

gauntlet (challenge)
(protective glove)

gill (breathing organ of a fish)
(small liquid measure)

gin (alcoholic beverage)
(apparatus for separating seeds from cotton)
(card game)

gore (blood)
(wound from a horn)
(three-sided insert of cloth)

grate (framework for burning fuel in a fireplace)
(have an annoying effect)

grave (place of burial)
(important; serious)
(carve)

graze (feed on grass)
(touch lightly in passing)

ground (soil)
(did grind)

grouse (game bird)
(grumble; complain)

gull (water bird)
(cheat; deceive)

gum (sticky substance from certain trees)
(tissue around teeth)

guy (rope; chain)
(fellow)

hack (cut roughly)
(carriage or car for hire)

hail (pieces of ice that fall like rain)
(shout of welcome)

hamper (hold back)
(large container or basket)

hatch (bring forth young from an egg)
(opening in a ship's deck)

hawk (bird of prey)
(peddle goods)

"The Reading Teacher's Book of Lists," © 1984 Prentice-Hall, Inc., Englewood Cliffs, NJ 07632. By E. Fry, J. Polk, and D. Fountoukidis."

haze (mist; smoke)
  (bully)

heel (back of the foot)
  (tip over to one side)

hide (conceal; keep out of sight)
  (animal skin)

hinder (stop)
  (rear)

hold (grasp and keep)
  (part of ship or plane for cargo)

husky (big and strong)
  (sled dog)

impress (have a strong effect on)
  (take by force)

incense (substance with a sweet smell
  when burned)
  (make very angry)

intern (force to stay)
  (doctor in training at a hospital)

intimate (very familiar)
  (suggest)

invalid (disabled person)
  (not valid)

jam (fruit preserve)
  (press or squeeze)

jar (container of glass)
  (rattle; vibrate)

jerky (with sudden starts and stops)
  (strips of dried meat)

jet (stream of water, steam, or air)
  (hard black coal)
  (type of airplane)

jig (dance)
  (fishing lure)

job (work)
Job (Biblical man of patience)

jumper (person or thing that jumps)
  (type of dress)

junk (trash)
  (Chinese sailing ship)

key (instrument for locking and
  unlocking)
  (low island)

kind (friendly; helpful)
  (same class)

lap (body part formed when sitting)
  (drink)
  (one course traveled)

lark (small songbird)
  (good fun)

lash (cord part of a whip)
  (tie or fasten)

last (at the end)
  (continue; endure)

launch (start out)
  (type of boat)

lead (show the way)
  (metallic element)

league (measure of distance)
  (group of persons or nations)

lean (stand slanting)
  (not fat)

leave (go away)
  (permission)

left (direction)
  (did leave)

lie (falsehood)
  (place oneself in a flat position;
  rest)

light (not heavy)
  (not dark)

like (similar to)
  (be pleased with)

"The Reading Teacher's Book of Lists, © 1984 Prentice-Hall, Inc., Englewood Cliffs, NJ 07632. By E. Fry, J. Polk, and D. Fountoukidis."

lime (citrus fruit)
    (chemical substance)

limp (lame walk)
    (not stiff)

line (piece of cord)
    (place paper or fabric inside)

list (series of words)
    (tilt to one side)

live (exist)
    (having life)

loaf (be idle)
    (shaped as bread)

lock (fasten door)
    (curl of hair)

long (great measure)
    (wish for)

loom (frame for weaving)
    (threaten)

lumber (timber)
    (move along heavily)

mace (club; weapon)
    (spice)

mail (letters)
    (flexible metal armor)

maroon (brownish red color)
    (leave helpless)

mat (woven floor covering)
    (border for picture)

match (stick used to light fires)
    (equal)

meal (food served at a certain time)
    (ground grain)

mean (signify; intend)
    (unkind)
    (average)

meter (unit of length)
    (poetic rhythm)
    (device that measures flow)

mine (belonging to me)
    (hole in the earth to get ores)

minute (60 seconds)
    (very small)

miss (fail to hit)
    (unmarried woman or girl)

mold (form; shape)
    (fungus)

mole (brown spot on the skin)
    (small underground animal)

mortar (cement mixture)
    (short cannon)

mount (high hill)
    (go up)

mow (cut down)
    (pile of hay or grain in a barn)

mule (cross between donkey and horse)
    (type of slipper)

mum (silent)
    (chrysanthemum)

nag (scold)
    (old horse)

nap (short sleep)
    (rug fuzz)

net (open-weave fabric)
    (remaining after deductions)

nip (small drink)
    (pinch)

pad (cushion)
    (walk softly)

page (one side of a sheet of paper)
    (youth who runs errands)

palm (inside of hand)
    (kind of tree)

patent (right or privilege)
    (type of leather)

patter (rapid taps)
    (light, easy walk)

pawn (leave as security for loan)
    (chess piece)

peaked (having a point)
    (looking ill)

peck (dry measure)
    (strike at)

pen (instrument for writing)
    (enclosed yard)

pile (heap or stack)
    (nap on fabrics)

pine (type of evergreen)
    (yearn or long for)

pitch (throw)
    (tar)

pitcher (container for pouring liquid)
    (baseball player)

poach (tresspass)
    (cook an egg)

poker (card game)
    (rod for stirring a fire)

pole (long piece of wood)
    (either end of the earth's axis)

policy (plan of action)
    (written agreement)

pool (tank with water)
    (game played with balls on a table)

pop (short, quick sound)
    (dad)
    (popular)

post (support)
    (job or position)
    (system for mail delivery)

pound (unit of weight)
    (hit hard again and again)
    (pen)

present (not absent)
    (gift)

press (squeeze)
    (force into service)

prime (chief)
    (prepare)

primer (first book)
    (something used to prepare another)

prune (fruit)
    (cut; trim)

pry (look with curiosity)
    (lift with force)

pump (type of shoe)
    (machine that forces liquid out)

punch (hit)
    (beverage)

pupil (student)
    (part of the eye)

quack (sound of a duck)
    (phony doctor)

racket (noise)
    (paddle used in tennis)

rail (bar of wood or metal)
    (complain bitterly)

rank (row or line)
    (having a bad odor)

rare (unusual)
    (not cooked much)

rash (hasty)
   (small red spots on the skin)

rear (the back part)
   (bring up)

ream (500 sheets of paper)
   (clean a hole)

recount (count again)
   (tell in detail)

reel (spool for winding)
   (sway under a blow)
   (lively dance)

refrain (hold back)
   (part repeated)

refuse (say no)
   (waste; trash)

rest (sleep)
   (what is left)

rifle (gun with a long barrel)
   (ransack; search through)

ring (circle)
   (bell sound)

root (underground part of a plant)
   (cheer for someone)

row (line)
   (use oars to move a boat)
   (noisy fight)

sage (wise person)
   (herb)

sap (liquid in a plant)
   (weaken)

sash (cloth worn around the waist)
   (frame of a window)

saw (did see)
   (tool for cutting)
   (wise saying)

scale (balance)
   (outer layer of fish and snakes)
   (series of steps)

school (place for learning)
   (group of fish)

scour (clean)
   (move quickly over)

scrap (small bits)
   (quarrel)

seal (mark of ownership)
   (sea mammal)

second (after the first)
   (one-sixtieth of a minute)

sewer (one who sews)
   (underground pipe for wastes)

shark (large meat-eating fish)
   (dishonest person)

shed (small shelter)
   (get rid of)

shingles (roofing materials)
   (viral disease)

shock (sudden violent disturbance)
   (thick busy mass)

shore (land near water's edge)
   (support)

shot (fired a gun)
   (worn out)

size (amount)
   (preparation of glue)

slaver (dealer in slaves)
   (salivate)

sledge (heavy sled)
   (large hammer)

slip (go easily)
   (small strip of paper)

slough (swamp)
(shed old skin)

slug (small slow-moving animal)
(hit hard)

smack (slight taste)
(open lips quickly)
(small boat)

snare (trap)
(strings on bottom of a drum)

snarl (growl)
(tangle)

sock (covering for foot)
(hit hard)

soil (ground; dirt)
(make dirty)

sole (type of fish)
(only)

sow (scatter seeds)
(pig)

spar (mast of a ship)
(argue)
(mineral)

spell (say the letters of a word)
(magic influence)
(period of work)

spray (sprinkle liquid)
(small branch with leaves and
flowers)

spruce (type of evergreen)
(neat or trim)

squash (press flat)
(vegetable)

stable (building for horses)
(unchanging)

stake (stick or post)
(risk or prize)

stalk (main stem of a plant)
(follow secretly)

stall (place in a stable for one animal)
(delay)

staple (metal fastener for paper)
(principal element)

stay (remain)
(support)

steep (having a sharp slope)
(soak)

steer (guide)
(young male cattle)

stem (part of a plant)
(stop; dam up)

stern (rear part of a ship)
(harsh; strict)

stick (thin piece of wood)
(pierce)

still (not moving)
(apparatus for making alcohol)

stoop (bend down)
(porch)

story (account of a happening)
(floor of a building)

strain (pull tight)
(group of individuals with an
inherited quality)

strand (leave helpless)
(thread or string)

strip (narrow piece of cloth)
(remove)

stroke (hit)
(pet; soothe)

stunt (stop growth)
(bold action)

sty (pen for pigs)
(swelling on eyelid)

swallow (take in)
(small bird)

tap (strike lightly)
(faucet)

tarry (delay)
(covered with tar)

tart (sour but agreeable)
(small fruit-filled pie)

tear (drop of liquid from the eye)
(pull apart)

temple (building for worship)
(side of forehead)

tend (incline to)
(take care of)

tender (not tough)
(offer)
(one who cares for)

tick (sound of a clock)
(small insect)
(pillow covering)

till (until)
(plow the land)
(drawer for money)

tip (end point)
(slant)
(present of money for services)

tire (become weary)
(rubber around a wheel)

toast (browned bread slices)
(wish for good luck)

toll (sound of a bell)
(fee paid for a privilege)

top (highest point)
(toy that spins)

troll (ugly dwarf)
(method of fishing)

unaffected (not influenced)
(innocent)

vault (storehouse for valuables)
(jump over)

vice (habit)
(clamp)

wake (stop sleeping)
(trail left behind a ship)

wax (substance made by bees)
(grow bigger)

well (satisfactory)
(hole dug for water)

whale (large sea mammal)
(whip)

will (statement of desire for
distribution of property after one's
death)
(is going to)
(deliberate intention or wish)

wind (air in motion)
(turn)

yak (long-haired ox)
(talk endlessly)

yard (enclosed space around a house)
(36 inches)

yen (strong desire)
(unit of money in Japan)

Near Misses—Words That Look Alike, Sound Alike, but Have Different Meanings

accept (*v.*)—agree to or take what is offered (I *accept* the job.)

except (*prep.*)—leaving out or excluding (Everyone went home *except* Janet.)

affect (*v.*)—have a result on; influence (The wind *affected* the instrument's accuracy.)

effect (*n.*)—the result of a cause (The *effect* of the earthquake was felt for miles.)

effect (*v.*)—make happen (Changes in the weather often *effect* changes in people's moods.)

alley (*n.*)—narrow street or path (The cat disappeared in the *alley*.)

ally (*n.*)—supporter; one united to another for a cause (France is an *ally* of the United States.)

all ready (*pron., adj.*)—completely prepared (We are *all ready* to go.)

already (*adv.*)—even now or by this time (John is *already* tired and it is still early.)

all together (*pron., adv.*)—everything or everyone gathered in one place (We were *all together* when we heard the terrible news.)

altogether (*adv.*)—entirely (There was *altogether* too much noise in the room.)

angel (*n.*)—heavenly being (The *angel* appeared to the wise men.)

angle (*n.*)—the space between two lines that meet in a point (Tom measured the *angle* with his protractor.)

anyway (*adv.*)—regardless (I'm going *anyway*. I don't care if it's snowing!)

any way (*adj., n.*)—in whatever manner (I'll get there *any way* I can.)

click (*n.*)—short sharp sound (We heard the *click* as the key turned in the lock.)

clique (*n.*)—small exclusive subgroup (The four girls formed a *clique* within the class.)

conscience (*n.*)—sense of right and wrong (His *conscience* bothered him after he lied.)

conscious (*adj.*)—aware; knowing (He was *conscious* of an intruder.)

contagious (*adj.*)—spread by contact (Measles is a *contagious* disease.)

contiguous (*adj.*)—touching or nearby (In the city we saw rows of *contiguous* houses.)

continually (*adv.*)—again and again (He *continually* loses umbrellas.)

"The Reading Teacher's Book of Lists, © 1984 Prentice-Hall, Inc., Englewood Cliffs, NJ 07632. By E. Fry, J. Polk, and D. Fountoukidis."

continuously (*adv.*)—unbroken; without a stop (The tape recording played *continuously.*)

costume (*n.*)—special way of dressing (We went in *costume* to the masquerade party.)

custom (*n.*)—usual practice or habit (It was his *custom* to read the paper at lunch.)

credible (*adj.*)—believable (He was a *credible* witness.)

creditable (*adj.*)—bringing honor to (She was our spokeswoman, and her behavior was *creditable.*)

credulous (*adj.*)—too ready to believe (The old woman was so *credulous* that children fooled her easily.

decease (*n.*)—death (The *decease* of the actor caused the film to be scrapped.)

disease (*n.*)—illness (The *disease* spread rapidly through the town.)

desert (*n.*)—arid land (The Gobi *Desert* is located in Mongolia.)

desert (*v.*)—abandon (The *deserted* town soon became a haven for outlaws.)

dessert (*n.*)—a course served at the end of a meal (We had apple pie for *dessert.*)

disinterested (*adj.*)—impartial (The judge was *disinterested* about the outcome of the trial.)

uninterested (*adj.*)—indifferent (He remained *uninterested* even after hearing about our profits.)

expect (*v.*)—suppose; look forward (I *expect* it to snow tonight.)

suspect (*v.*)—imagine to be; mistrust (I *suspect* he had a good reason for leaving so early.)

farther (*adj.*)—more distant (Carol swam *farther* than Alice.)

further (*adj.*)—extending beyond a point (Because he wanted to *further* his career he went to night school.)

formally (*adj.*)—with rigid ceremonies (We addressed the ambassador *formally.*)

formerly (*adv.*)—previously (*Formerly* we had invited only recent graduates; now we invite all alumni.)

later (*adv.*)—after a particular time (We'll talk *later,* after we have some rest.)

latter (*adj.*)—more recent (After considering the two demonstrations, I feel the *latter* was more effective.)

least (*adj.*)—at the minimum ("It's the *least* I could do," he said.)

"The Reading Teacher's Book of Lists, © 1984 Prentice-Hall, Inc., Englewood Cliffs, NJ 07632. By E. Fry, J. Polk, and D. Fountoukidis."

lest (*conj.*)—for fear that (We'd better attend the meeting *lest* our manager become angry.)

loose (*adj.*)—not tight (The string on the package was *loose.*)

lose (*v.*)—not win; misplace (It was a real disappointment to *lose* the game.)

maybe (*adv.*)—perhaps (*Maybe* we can fix the leak.)

may be (*v.*)—is possible that (That *may be* the restaurant he told us about.)

moral (*n.*)—lesson; ethic (The *moral* of the fable was not easy to understand.)

morale (*n.*)—mental and emotional condition (The *morale* of the group was bolstered by the news.)

of (*prep.*)—having to do with; indicating possession (The rim *of* the cup was chipped.)

off (*adv.*)—not on (We wandered *off* the path several times.)

persecute (*v.*)—harass, annoy, or injure (The ruler was known to *persecute* anyone who disagreed with him.)

prosecute (*n.*)—press for punishment for a crime (The attorney will tell us if he can *prosecute* the alleged thief.)

personal (*adj.*)—relating to a person individually (Tom refused the invitation for *personal* reasons.)

personnel (*n.*)—employees (The memo stated that all *personnel* must register on Saturdays.)

picture (*n.*)—drawing or photograph (I bought a frame for that *picture* today.)

pitcher (*n.*)—container for liquid; baseball player (She filled the *pitcher* with ice.)

preposition (*n.*)—part of speech (The words *to, of,* and *by* are *prepositions.*)

proposition (*n.*)—proposal or suggestion (We were suspicious of his *proposition.*)

quiet (*adj.*)—silent; not noisy (The children were all *quiet.*)

quite (*adv.*)—very (We were *quite* disturbed by the news of the accident.)

respectfully (*adv.*)—having respect for (He answered his grandfather *respectfully.*)

respectively (*adv.*)—in the order given (Mary and Sue are 16 and 18, *respectively.*)

suppose (*v.*)—assume or imagine (*Suppose* you and I were very old; what would it be like?)

supposed (*adj.*)—expected (Tom was *supposed* to go, not I.)

than (*conj.*)—word used to compare (Georgia is taller *than* Sally.)

"The Reading Teacher's Book of Lists, © 1984 Prentice-Hall, Inc., Englewood Cliffs, NJ 07632. By E. Fry, J. Polk, and D. Fountoukidis."

then (*adv.*)—next in order of time (First the bell rang; *then* the children lined up.)

use (*v.*)—employ something (I had to *use* my key because the door was locked.)

used (*adj.*)—secondhand (Karen bought a *used* car.)

Related Actions—These Near Misses Often Have a Linking Concept

aggravate (*v.*)—make worse or anger
agitate (*v.*)—stir up or arouse feelings

emigrate (*v.*)—leave the country of one's residence
immigrate (*v.*)—enter a new country to reside there

imply (*v.*)—express indirectly
infer (*v.*)—derive a conclusion from indirect evidence

lay (*v.*)—set something down or place something
lie (*v.*)—be or stay at rest

leave (*v.*)—go away from; permission
let (*v.*)—allow; permit

set (*v.*)—place something
sit (*v.*)—take a resting position on a chair

INSTANT WORDS

These are the 1,000 most commonly used words in the English language. The first 100 (including their variations) make up about 50 percent of all written material, and the whole 1,000 make up about 90 percent of all written material. Obviously, children should be taught to recognize them instantly.

This list is taken directly from *3000 Instant Words*, by Elizabeth Sakiey and Edward Fry (1979, Dreier Educational Systems, Highland Park, NJ. Now available from Jamestown Publications, Providence, RI.) The words are ranked in order of frequency of occurrence. The *3000 Instant Words* book gives more information about these words, an alphabetical arrangement, and the frequency of the common suffixes.

These words can be taught with flash cards, in games like Pairs and Bingo (see section VI of this book for some games), in spelling lessons, and in many other ways. This is a valuable and well-researched list of words.

1. the	25. from	49. their	73. write
2. of	26. or	50. if	74. go
3. and	27. one	51. will	75. see
4. a	28. had	52. up	76. number
5. to	29. by	53. other	77. no
6. in	30. words	54. about	78. way
7. is	31. but	55. out	79. could
8. you	32. not	56. many	80. people
9. that	33. what	57. then	81. my
10. it	34. all	58. them	82. than
11. he	35. were	59. these	83. first
12. was	36. we	60. so	84. water
13. for	37. when	61. some	85. been
14. on	38. your	62. her	86. called
15. are	39. can	63. would	87. who
16. as	40. said	64. make	88. oil
17. with	41. there	65. like	89. its
18. his	42. use	66. him	90. now
19. they	43. an	67. into	91. find
20. I	44. each	68. time	92. long
21. at	45. which	69. has	93. down
22. be	46. she	70. look	94. day
23. this	47. do	71. two	95. did
24. have	48. how	72. more	96. get

97. come	138. any	179. picture	220. eyes
98. made	139. same	180. again	221. light
99. may	140. tell	181. change	222. thought
100. part	141. boy	182. off	223. head
101. over	142. following	183. play	224. under
102. new	143. came	184. spell	225. story
103. sound	144. want	185. air	226. saw
104. take	145. show	186. away	227. left
105. only	146. also	187. animals	228. don't
106. little	147. around	188. house	229. few
107. work	148. form	189. point	230. while
108. know	149. three	190. page	231. along
109. place	150. small	191. letters	232. might
110. years	151. set	192. mother	233. close
111. live	152. put	193. answer	234. something
112. me	153. end	194. found	235. seemed
113. back	154. does	195. study	236. next
114. give	155. another	196. still	237. hard
115. most	156. well	197. learn	238. open
116. very	157. large	198. should	239. example
117. after	158. must	199. American	240. beginning
118. things	159. big	200. world	241. life
119. our	160. even	201. high	242. always
120. just	161. such	202. every	243. those
121. name	162. because	203. near	244. both
122. good	163. turned	204. add	245. paper
123. sentence	164. here	205. food	246. together
124. man	165. why	206. between	247. got
125. think	166. asked	207. own	248. group
126. say	167. went	208. below	249. often
127. great	168. men	209. country	250. run
128. where	169. read	210. plants	251. important
129. help	170. need	211. last	252. until
130. through	171. land	212. school	253. children
131. much	172. different	213. father	254. side
132. before	173. home	214. keep	255. feet
133. line	174. us	215. trees	256. car
134. right	175. move	216. never	257. miles
135. too	176. try	217. started	258. night
136. means	177. kind	218. city	259. walked
137. old	178. hand	219. earth	260. white

261. sea	302. music	343. products	384. notice
262. began	303. color	344. happened	385. south
263. grow	304. stand	345. whole	386. sing
264. took	305. sun	346. measure	387. war
265. river	306. questions	347. remember	388. ground
266. four	307. fish	348. early	389. fall
267. carry	308. area	349. waves	390. king
268. state	309. mark	350. reached	391. town
269. once	310. dog	351. listen	392. I'll
270. book	311. horse	352. wind	393. unit
271. hear	312. birds	353. rock	394. figure
272. stop	313. problem	354. space	395. certain
273. without	314. complete	355. covered	396. field
274. second	315. room	356. fast	397. travel
275. later	316. knew	357. several	398. wood
276. miss	317. since	358. hold	399. fire
277. idea	318. ever	359. himself	400. upon
278. enough	319. piece	360. toward	401. done
279. eat	320. told	361. five	402. English
280. face	321. usually	362. step	403. road
281. watch	322. didn't	363. morning	404. half
282. far	323. friends	364. passed	405. ten
283. Indians	324. easy	365. vowel	406. fly
284. really	325. heard	366. true	407. gave
285. almost	326. order	367. hundred	408. box
286. let	327. red	368. against	409. finally
287. above	328. door	369. pattern	410. wait
288. girl	329. sure	370. numeral	411. correct
289. sometimes	330. become	371. table	412. oh
290. mountains	331. top	372. north	413. quickly
291. cut	332. ship	373. slowly	414. person
292. young	333. across	374. money	415. became
293. talk	334. today	375. map	416. shown
294. soon	335. during	376. farm	417. minutes
295. list	336. short	377. pulled	418. strong
296. song	337. better	378. draw	419. verb
297. being	338. best	379. voice	420. stars
298. leave	339. however	380. seen	421. front
299. family	340. low	381. cold	422. feel
300. it's	341. hours	382. cried	423. fact
301. body	342. black	383. plan	424. inches

425. street	466. though	507. felt	548. wall
426. decided	467. language	508. suddenly	549. forest
427. contain	468. shape	509. test	550. probably
428. course	469. deep	510. direction	551. legs
429. surface	470. thousands	511. center	552. sat
430. produce	471. yes	512. farmers	553. main
431. building	472. clear	513. ready	554. winter
432. ocean	473. equation	514. anything	555. wide
433. class	474. yet	515. divided	556. written
434. note	475. government	516. general	557. length
435. nothing	476. filled	517. energy	558. reason
436. rest	477. heat	518. subject	559. kept
437. carefully	478. full	519. Europe	560. interest
438. scientists	479. hot	520. moon	561. arms
439. inside	480. check	521. region	562. brother
440. wheels	481. object	522. return	563. race
441. stay	482. am	523. believe	564. present
442. green	483. rule	524. dance	565. beautiful
443. known	484. among	525. members	566. store
444. island	485. noun	526. picked	567. job
445. week	486. power	527. simple	568. edge
446. less	487. cannot	528. cells	569. past
447. machine	488. able	529. paint	570. sign
448. base	489. six	530. mind	571. record
449. ago	490. size	531. love	572. finished
450. stood	491. dark	532. cause	573. discovered
451. plane	492. ball	533. rain	574. wild
452. system	493. material	534. exercise	575. happy
453. behind	494. special	535. eggs	576. beside
454. ran	495. heavy	536. train	577. gone
455. round	496. fine	537. blue	578. sky
456. boat	497. pair	538. wish	579. glass
457. game	498. circle	539. drop	580. million
458. force	499. include	540. developed	581. west
459. brought	500. built	541. window	582. lay
460. understand	501. can't	542. difference	583. weather
461. warm	502. matter	543. distance	584. root
462. common	503. square	544. heart	585. instruments
463. bring	504. syllables	545. sit	586. meet
464. explain	505. perhaps	546. sum	587. third
465. dry	506. bill	547. summer	588. months

589. paragraph	630. bed	671. speed	712. England
590. raised	631. copy	672. count	713. burning
591. represent	632. free	673. cat	714. design
592. soft	633. hope	674. someone	715. joined
593. whether	634. spring	675. sail	716. foot
594. clothes	635. case	676. rolled	717. law
595. flowers	636. laughed	677. bear	718. ears
596. shall	637. nation	678. wonder	719. grass
597. teacher	638. quite	679. smiled	720. you're
598. held	639. type	680. angle	721. grew
599. describe	640. themselves	681. fraction	722. skin
600. drive	641. temperature	682. Africa	723. valley
601. cross	642. bright	683. killed	724. cents
602. speak	643. lead	684. melody	725. key
603. solve	644. everyone	685. bottom	726. president
604. appear	645. method	686. trip	727. brown
605. metal	646. section	687. hole	728. trouble
606. son	647. lake	688. poor	729. cool
607. either	648. consonant	689. let's	730. cloud
608. ice	649. within	690. fight	731. lost
609. sleep	650. dictionary	691. surprise	732. sent
610. village	651. hair	692. French	733. symbols
611. factors	652. age	693. died	734. wear
612. result	653. amount	694. beat	735. bad
613. jumped	654. scale	695. exactly	736. save
614. snow	655. pounds	696. remain	737. experiment
615. ride	656. although	697. dress	738. engine
616. care	657. per	698. iron	739. alone
617. floor	658. broken	699. couldn't	740. drawing
618. hill	659. moment	700. fingers	741. east
619. pushed	660. tiny	701. row	742. pay
620. baby	661. possible	702. least	743. single
621. buy	662. gold	703. catch	744. touch
622. century	663. milk	704. climbed	745. information
623. outside	664. quiet	705. wrote	746. express
624. everything	665. natural	706. shouted	747. mouth
625. tall	666. lot	707. continued	748. yard
626. already	667. stone	708. itself	749. equal
627. instead	668. act	709. else	750. decimal
628. phrase	669. build	710. plains	751. yourself
629. soil	670. middle	711. gas	752. control

753. practice	794. hunting	835. indicate	876. major
754. report	795. flow	836. except	877. observe
755. straight	796. lady	837. expect	878. tube
756. rise	797. students	838. flat	879. necessary
757. statement	798. human	839. seven	880. weight
758. stick	799. art	840. interesting	881. meat
759. party	800. feeling	841. sense	882. lifted
760. seeds	801. supply	842. string	883. process
761. suppose	802. corner	843. blow	884. army
762. woman	803. electric	844. famous	885. hat
763. coast	804. insects	845. value	886. property
764. bank	805. crops	846. wings	887. particular
765. period	806. tone	847. movement	888. swim
766. wire	807. hit	848. pole	889. terms
767. choose	808. sand	849. exciting	890. current
768. clean	809. doctor	850. branches	891. park
769. visit	810. provide	851. thick	892. sell
770. bit	811. thus	852. blood	893. shoulder
771. whose	812. won't	853. lie	894. industry
772. received	813. cook	854. spot	895. wash
773. garden	814. bones	855. bell	896. block
774. please	815. tail	856. fun	897. spread
775. strange	816. board	857. loud	898. cattle
776. caught	817. modern	858. consider	899. wife
777. fell	818. compound	859. suggested	900. sharp
778. team	819. mine	860. thin	901. company
779. God	820. wasn't	861. position	902. radio
780. captain	821. fit	862. entered	903. we'll
781. direct	822. addition	863. fruit	904. action
782. ring	823. belong	864. tied	905. capital
783. serve	824. safe	865. rich	906. factories
784. child	825. soldiers	866. dollars	907. settled
785. desert	826. guess	867. send	908. yellow
786. increase	827. silent	868. sight	909. isn't
787. history	828. trade	869. chief	910. southern
788. cost	829. rather	870. Japanese	911. truck
789. maybe	830. compare	871. stream	912. fair
790. business	831. crowd	872. planets	913. printed
791. separate	832. poem	873. rhythm	914. wouldn't
792. break	833. enjoy	874. eight	915. ahead
793. uncle	834. elements	875. science	916. chance

917. born	938. shop	959. allow	980. nor
918. level	939. suffix	960. fear	981. rope
919. triangle	940. especially	961. workers	982. cotton
920. molecules	941. shoes	962. Washington	983. apple
921. France	942. actually	963. Greek	984. details
922. repeated	943. nose	964. women	985. entire
923. column	944. afraid	965. bought	986. corn
924. western	945. dead	966. led	987. substances
925. church	946. sugar	967. march	988. smell
926. sister	947. adjective	968. northern	989. tools
927. oxygen	948. fig	969. create	990. conditions
928. plural	949. office	970. British	991. cows
929. various	950. huge	971. difficult	992. track
930. agreed	951. gun	972. match	993. arrived
931. opposite	952. similar	973. win	994. located
932. wrong	953. death	974. doesn't	995. sir
933. chart	954. score	975. steel	996. seat
934. prepared	955. forward	976. total	997. division
935. pretty	956. stretched	977. deal	998. effect
936. solution	957. experience	978. determine	999. underline
937. fresh	958. rose	979. evening	1000. view

WORDS USED IN DIFFERENT SCHOOL SUBJECTS

If students are doing poorly in a subject in school, perhaps they can't read the words used to teach that subject. Try them out on one of these lists. If they can't read or don't know the meanings of too many of the words, then perhaps insufficient vocabulary is contributing to the low grades.

Conversely, in preparing students to read in certain subject areas, helping them develop some familiarity with the words used is a good start.

We haven't covered all of the subjects taught in schools, but the Mathematics, Social Studies, and Science lists presented here are a good start. The grade-level designations are not to be taken too exactly, but *primary* tends to mean the first three grades, *intermediate* is grades 4 through 8, and *secondary* is grades 9 through 12.

Mathematics Vocabulary—Primary

A
add
addend
addition
alike
all
amount
angle
Arabic numerals
area
array
associative property
average

B
base
base ten
between
both

C
calendar
cent
center

centimeter
change
circle
circumference
column
combine
common factor
common multiple
commutative property
compare
compass
composite number
compute
cone
congruent
connect
contain
corner
cost
count
counting numbers
cube
curve
cylinder

D
decimal
degree
denominator
diagonal
diameter
difference
digit
dime
distance
distributive property
divide
dividend
divisor
dollar
double
dozen

E
each
element
empty set
end point
equal

equation
equivalent
estimate
even number
expanded numeral

F

fact
factor
fewer
figure
foot, feet
fraction

G

gallon
geometry
gram
graph
greater than
grid
group

H

half
height
hexagon
horizontal
hour

I

identify
inch
inequality
infinite set
inside
instead
intersect

J

join

K

kilogram
kilometer

L

least
length
less
line
liter

M

many
match
mathemetics
measure
median
member
metric
middle
mile
minuend
minus
minute
missing
mixed
model
money
more
most
multiple
multiplication

N

name
natural order
negative
nickel
number
number line
numerator

O

object
octagon
odd
one-to-one
open
operation
opposite
order
ordinal
ounce

P

pair
parallel
parallelogram
parenthesis, parentheses
pattern
penny
pentagon
percent
perimeter
perpendicular
place holder
place value
plane
plus
point
polygon
positive
pound
prime number
principle
problem
product
property
probability
protractor
pyramid

"*The Reading Teacher's Book of Lists,* © 1984 Prentice-Hall, Inc., Englewood Cliffs, NJ 07632. By E. Fry, J. Polk, and D. Fountoukidis."

Q

quadrilateral
quart
quotient

R

radius
range
ratio
ray
reciprocal
rectangle
regroup
related facts
remainder
rename
rhombus
right angle
Roman numeral
round
row

S

same
score
second
segment
sequence
set

shaded
shape
short form
side
sign
similar
simple
single
size
solution
solve
some
space
sphere
square
standard numeral
straight
subset
subtract
subtrahend
sum
symbol
symmetrical

T

table
temperature
thermometer
time

times
ton
total
triangle

U

unequal
union
unit
unknown
unnamed

V

value
vertex
vertical
volume

W

week
weight
whole number
width

Y

yard

Z

zero

Mathematics Vocabulary—Intermediate

A

abscissa
absolute value
acre
actual
acute angle
acute triangle

additive
additive inverse
adjacent
alternate
altitude
approximately
arc
arithmetic mean

avoirdupois
axis

B

baker's dozen
bar graph
base five
base two

basic facts
billion
binary operation
bisect
broken-line graph

C

calculate
capacity
cardinal
caret
cast out
Celsius
centigrade
centigram
centiliter
central angle
century
circle graph
circumscribe
clock arithmetic
closed curve
closure
commission
common denominator
comparison
complex
computation
concentric
consecutive
constant
construct
convert
coordinate axis
corresponding
cross-product
cross-section
cubed
cubic
currency

D

data
decade
decimal point
decrease
deposit
depth
derive
determine
diagram
dimension
discount
denominator
diagonal
diameter
divisibility
division
dot graph
dry measure
duplicate

E

equality
equiangular triangle
equilateral triangle
error of measurement
estimation
exact
expanded
experiment
exponent
exponential notation
express
extend
exterior

F

face
face value

factor tree
factorial
Fahrenheit
family of facts
finite
fixed
fluid ounce
foci
foot-pound
formula
frequency
frequency table

G

generalization
given
graduated scale
graph of the equation
greatest common factor
greatest possible multiple
gross
gross weight

H

hemisphere
histogram

I

identity property
imply
improper fraction
include
inclusion
increase
inference
input
integer
interest rate
interior
interpret

"The Reading Teacher's Book of Lists, © 1984 Prentice-Hall, Inc., Englewood Cliffs, NJ 07632. By E. Fry, J. Polk, and D. Fountoukidis."

intersection
interval
inverse
isosceles triangle

K

kiloliter

L

lateral
least common denominator
least common factor
least common multiple
leg of a triangle
linear
line graph
line of symmetry
line segment
lowest terms

M

magic square
markup
matching
maximum
mean
meter stick
micron
midway
minimum
mixed numeral
mode
month
multiplicand
multiplier

N

natural number
negative number
notation

numeral
numeration
numeration system

O

obtuse angle
odd number
open equation
open figure
open sentence
ordered pairs
origin
outcome
output

P

partial
per
perfect number
period
pi
pictograph
plane figure
plot
power
precision
predict
prime factor
procedure
profit
progression
proper fraction
proportion
Pythagorean theorem

Q

quadrant
quantity

R

radian
radii
ranking
rate
rational number
reduce
reflexive property
regular
repeating decimal
restriction
reverse
right triangle

S

satisfies
scale drawing
scalene triangle
scientific notation
sector
semicircle
short division
simplest terms
simplify
skew lines
skip counting
solid
squared
square feet
square inches
square meter
square mile
square root
standard
statute mile
story problem
straight angle
straight edge
subscript
substitute

subtraction
successive
super set
supplementary angle
surface area
system

T

tablespoon
tally
tangent
teaspoon
terminate
terms
theorem
transitive property

trapezoid
trial
triple
two-dimensional

U

undivided
union of sets
universal set
unlimited
unmatched
upper limit

V

variable
vertical angle
vertical axis

W

word problem

X

x-axis

Y

yardstick
y-axis
yearly

Social Studies Vocabulary—Intermediate

A

abolish
abolitionist
aborigine
absolute power
administration
alien
alliance
ally
amnesty
amendment
ancestor
ancient
anthropology
archeology
aristocracy
artifact
assembly
authority
autocracy
automation
average

B

balance of power
barbarian
barter
bill
bloc
blockade
bourgeois
boycott
bureaucracy

C

cabinet
candidate
capitalism
charter
city
civil
civilization
civil war
colony
communist

compromise
confederation
Congress
Constitution

D

debate
declaration
delegate
demarcation
democracy
depression
dictator
diplomat
disarmament
discrimination
divine right

E

ecology
ecosystem
election

emancipate
embargo
emigration
emperor
executive branch
exile
expedition
explorer

F

fact
federal
feudal
foreign
freedom
frontier

G

generation
government
governor
group

H

heritage
history
homestead
humanitarian

I

immigrant
impeach
imperialism
inaugurate
indentured servant
independence
Industrial Revolution
invention

J

judicial branch
jury
justice

L

labor union
law
legal
legislative branch

M

majority
mandate
manufacturing
mayor
medieval
mercantilism
migrant
military
minority
missionary
monarchy
monopoly
monotheism

N

nationalism
neutrality
nobility
nomination

O

official
oligarchy
oligopoly
oppression
oracle
organization

P

Parliament
patriot
peasant
per capita income
persecute
petition
pharaoh
pilgrim
pioneer
planned economic system
political
political process
politics
policy
polytheism
pope
possession
prehistoric
prejudice
president
primary
prime minister
primitive
proclamation
prohibit

propaganda
public opinion
puritan

R

radical
ratify
Reconstruction
referendum
reform
Reformation
refugee
renaissance
represent
representative
republic
republican
reservation
residential
resolution
revenue
revolt
revolution
Revolutionary War
royalist
rule

S

sanction
secession
segregation
senator
serf
settlement
sharecropper
shogun
siege
slavery
socialist
social scientist
society

sociology
sovereignty
state
strike
system

T

tariff
taxation
technology

territories
theory
time line
tolerance
totalitarian
trade
traditional
trait
traitor
treason

treaty
truce
tyranny
tyrant

U

unanimous
unconstitutional
union
unite

V

vassal
veteran
veto
viceroy
volunteer

W

warfare
worship

Social Studies Vocabulary—Secondary

A

acculturation
acre
affluent
agriculture
alluvial
altitude
Antarctic Circle
anthracite
apartheid
aqueduct
arable
archipelago
Arctic Circle
artesian well
atmosphere
atomic energy
axis

B

basin
bay
bazaar
Bedouins
birth rate
bituminous
boundary

C

canal
canneries
capital
cartographer
cash crop
Caucasian
cellulose
century
chaparral
climate
cistern
citrus fruit
civil rights
coast
code
cold war
collective farm
colonialism
colonization
commercial farming
Common Market
commonwealth
commune
communism
competition
condensation level

coniferous
conquistador
conservation
consumer goods
continent
continental divide
convection process
cooperative
country
craftsmen
crop rotation
crude oil
culture
current
czar

D

dam
death rate
deciduous
degree
delta
demographer
density of population
desalinization
desert
dew point

dictatorship
dike
doldrums
dust storm
dynasty

E

earth
earthquake
electricity
elevation
empire
environment
equal-area map
equator
equinox
erosion
erratics
estuary
evaporation
export

F

fiord
flash flood
flood plain
flow resources

"The Reading Teacher's Book of Lists, © 1984 Prentice-Hall, Inc., Englewood Cliffs, NJ 07632. By E. Fry, J. Polk, and D. Fountoukidis."

foreign policy
fossil
fossil fuels
freeway
Free World
fund resources

G

gaucho
geography
geologist
ghetto
glacier
globe
grassland
greenhouse effect
grid
gross national product
growing season
gulf
Gulf Stream

H

harbor
heavy industry
hemisphere
herbicide
herdsman
highland
high latitude
highrise apartment
horticulture
humidity
hydroelectric

I

ice cap
Ice Age
illiteracy
industrial region

insecticide
International Date Line
investment
Iron Curtain
irrigation
island
isthmus

J

jet stream
jungle

K

kibbutz

L

lake
landlocked
leaching
legend
legislature
life expectancy
light industry
lines of latitude
lines of longitude
literacy
lowland
low latitudes

M

magistrate
marine climate
market
maritime
mass production
megalopolis
Mercator map
merchant
meridian
meteorologist
metropolis

metropolitan area
middle class
Middle East
middle latitudes
migratory farming
migratory workers
mineral
minority groups
missile
Mongoloid
monsoon
moraine
Moslem
mosque
mother country

N

natural resources
Near East
nomad
North Atlantic Treaty
  Organization
North Pole

O

oasis
ocean
ocean current
open-housing laws
orbit
Orient
outback

P

papyrus
parallel
party line
peninsula
peon
petrified
physical

"The Reading Teacher's Book of Lists, © 1984 Prentice-Hall, Inc., Englewood Cliffs, NJ 07632. By E. Fry, J. Polk, and D. Fountoukidis."

pilgrimage
plain
plantation
plateau
polar map
pollution
population density
prairie
precipitation
Prime Meridian

R

rainfall
rain forest
ration
raw materials
reclamation
refine
reincarnation
relief map
renewable resource
reserves

reservoir
river
river mouth
river source
rotation
rural

S

satellite country
savannah
scale of miles
sea level
sediment
seismograph
sheik
Shinto
slum
smelting
smog
South Pole
Soviet
statistics

steppe
strait
subsistence farming
subtropical
suburb
surplus

T

tableland
temperature
tenant
tenement
textile
tidal wave
topography
topsoil
tributary
Tropic of Cancer
Tropic of Capricorn
tsetse fly
tundra
typhoon

U

underdeveloped
United Nations
urban
urban blight
urban revolution

V

valley
vertical climate
volcano

W

warm front
water power
watershed
water vapor
weather

Z

zone
zoologist

Geography Vocabulary—Intermediate

A

acre
adapt
agriculture
altitude
antarctic
arable
archipelago
arctic
area
arid
Asia
atmosphere
autonomy
axis

B

balance
barren
barter
basin
bay
bayou
beliefs
belt
Bering Strait
blizzard
boundary
branch
broadleaf
burgher

C

canal
canyons
cape
capital
census
central
cliff
climate
coast
commercial
communal
community
compass
country

continent
continental divide
contour
cottage industry
country
county
crater
crops
crust
cultivation
cultural region
culture
current
customs
cyclone

D

data
death rate
deciduous
degree
delta
density
desert
developing nation
diagram
dialect
direction
distance
diversity
domestic
drought
dust bowl

E

earthquake
east
eastern hemisphere
eclipse
ecology
economy
elevation
emigration
empire
environment
epidemic
equator
equinox
erosion
estuary
ethnic
Europe
evergreen
export

F

famine
fathom
fault
fertile
fiord
fishery
foliage
fossil
freight
fuel

G

geography
geyser
glacier
globe
goods
grain
graph
grasslands
gravity
great circle
Great Plains
grid
gross national product
gulf

H

harbor
harvest
hemisphere
hinterland
horizon
humidity
hurricane
hydroelectric

I

iceberg
ice cap
import
income
industry

inland
inlet
international waters
irrigation
island
isolated
isthmus

J

jet stream
jungle

K

kilometer
knot

L

lake
lagoon
latitude
lava
legend
levee
level
life expectancy
literacy
longitude
lowlands

M

mainland
manufacture
map
marine
marsh
mass
meadow
Mediterranean
megalopolis
meridian

mesa
meters
metropolitan area
migrant
moderate
monarchy
monsoon
mountain
mouth of a river

N

nation
nationalism
nationality
native
natural
natural resources
navigable
navigation
neighborhood
neutral
nomad
nonrenewable resource
North Pole

O

oasis
occidental
ocean
oceanography
orbit
ore
oriental
overpopulation

P

parallel
pasture
peak
peninsula

petroleum
physical map
plain
planet
plateau
polar
pollution
population density
port
prairie
precipice
precipitation

R

rainfall
rain forest
range
rapids
raw materials
reef
refinery
region
relief
religion
renewable resource
resources
reservoir
residential area
resort
river
rotation
route
rural

S

savannah
scale
sea
season
semiarid
silt

smog
solar
South Pole
sphere
standard of living
steppe
strait
suburb
supply
surplus
survey
swamp

T

technology
temperature
terracing
tidal wave
tide
tidewater
timberline
time line
trade
tributary
tropic
tundra

U

universal
urban

V

valley
vast
vegetation
vernacular
vertical
vital statistics
volcano
voyage

W

waterpower
weather
Western Hemisphere
wharf

whirlpool
wilderness
windmill

Z

zone

History Vocabulary—Secondary

A

abolitionist
absolute monarchy
AFL-CIO
age
aggressor
alien
alliance
Allied Powers
ally
amendment
American Federation
of Labor
American Revolution
ancestors
annex
appointed
armistice
arsenal
Articles of
Confederation
artifact
assassinate
assembly
automation
average
Axis Powers

B

balance
bill
Bill of Rights
birth rate

blockade
bonds
boom
bootleg
boundaries
boycott

C

cabinet
campaign
capitalism
captains of industry
carpetbaggers
caucus
cede
census
Central Powers
century
charter
checks and balances
civilization
civil rights
civil war
cold war
collective bargaining
colony
commerce
communism
communities
compromise
concentration camps
confederacy
conflicts

Congress
Congress of Industrial
Organizations
conquer
conquistador
conservation
conservative
Constitution
consumer
continents
contraband
convention
convert
corporation
crisis
Crusades
culture
currency
customs

D

Dark Ages
debts
declare
defense
delegates
democracy
density of population
deposits
depression
desegregation
dictators
discovery

"The Reading Teacher's Book of Lists, © 1984 Prentice-Hall, Inc., Englewood Cliffs, NJ 07632. By E. Fry, J. Polk, and D. Fountoukidis."

discrimination
dissent
divorce
document
draft
duty

E

ecology
economy
effigy
elastic clause
elector
electoral vote
emancipation
embargo
emigration
empire
energy
enforced
environment
equality
ethnic
excise
executive
expedition
exploration
export

F

factory
Far East
fascism
favored
federal
Federalist
Federal Reserve System
feminist
filibuster
fleet
foreign

founded
freed
free enterprise
frontier

G

gangsters
generation
geography
ghetto
glacier
government
granges
greenbacks
growth

H

habeas corpus
harvesting
heritage
homestead
House of Representatives
housing
hypothesis

I

illegal
immigration
impeach
import
inaugurate
income
income tax
indentured servant
independence
industrial
Industrial Revolution
inflation
influenced
injunction
integration

invasion
invention
invested
investigation
Iron Curtain
irrigate
Islam
isolationism

J

judiciary
jury
justice

K

kidnapped
knowledge
Ku Klux Klan

L

labor
labor union
lack
laissez faire
Latin America
legislature
League of Nations
leisure
liberal
life expectancy
limits
local
lockout
loyalist
lynching

M

Manifest Destiny
manufacture
martial law
mass production

materials
Mayflower Compact
megalopolis
merchant
metropolitan area
migrant
migration
military
militia
mineral
minimum
minority
minutemen
missile
missionary
moderates
modern
monopoly
Monroe Doctrine
Moslems
movement
muckrakers
museum

N

nationalism
Nazism
negotiate
neutral
nobles
nomad
nominate
nonviolence
North Atlantic Treaty
  Organization
nuclear weapons
null and void

O

occupied
officials

opinion
opportunity
opposed
organization

P

pacifists
Parliament
passage
patent
patriot
patriotism
peasant
petition
pilgrim
pioneer
plantation
platform
pocket veto
political party
politician
poll tax
pollution
population
possessions
postwar
poverty
practices
preamble
precedent
prehistory
prejudice
primary
profit
progressive
prohibition
promotion
propaganda
property
prospector
protest

Protestant
provision
public works
Puritans

R

radicals
ratify
ration
raw materials
reapportionment
rebellion
rebels
recession
reconstruction
recovery
recreation
referendum
refineries
reform
regions
regulation
religion
relocation centers
remains
repeal
representatives
republic
reservations
reservoirs
resign
resources
retreat
revolution
riots
ruins
rural

S

sabotage
satellite

scandal
secede
secession
segregate
Selective Service Act
Senate
seniority
separation of powers
serf
settlements
sharecropper
shortage
slavery
smuggling
socialists
social security
spoils system
standard of living
stock
stockade
stock market
strategy
strike
suburbs
surrender

survive
sweatshops

T

tariff
taxation
technology
telegraph
tenant
tenement
territory
tolerate
town meeting
traditional
trails
traitors
transcontinental
treason
treaty
trend
trial
tribes
troops
truce

U

unanimous
underdeveloped
underground railroad
union
United Nations
unskilled worker
urban revolution

V

veteran
veto
violence
vocational
voyage

W

wages
war hawks
warrant
welfare
wilderness
worship
worker's compensation

Science Vocabulary—Elementary

A
abdomen
absorb
accurate
adaptation
air current
air pressure
algae
amoeba
amphibian
ancestor
apply
astronaut

astronomer
atmosphere

B

backbone
bacteria
balance
barometer
battery
behavior
blood vessels
boil
breathe

C
calcium
capillary
carbohydrate
carbon dioxide
cartilage
cell
Celsius
census
centimeter
chemical
chlorine
chlorophyll

circuit
circulation
classify
climate
cloud
community
compass
compound
concave
condense
conductor
constant
constellation

continent
contract
control
convection
convex
core
crust
current

D

decay
decompose
degree

"*The Reading Teacher's Book of Lists*, © 1984 Prentice-Hall, Inc., Englewood Cliffs, NJ 07632. By E. Fry, J. Polk, and D. Fountoukidis."

density
desert
dew
diaphragm
diatom
digestion
dinosaur
disease
dissolve
distance

E

ear
ear drum
earth
earthworm
echo
eclipse
egg
electricity
embryo
energy
environment
equator
erosion
esophagus
evaporate
evidence
expand
extinct

F

Fahrenheit
fat
fern
fertile
fertilizer
filament
flood
flow

flower
focus
fog
food chain
force
fossil
friction
frost
fruit
fuel
funnel

G

gas
geyser
gills
glacier
grain
gravity

H

habitat
hail
hatch
heat
hemisphere
hibernate
horizon
humus
hurricane

I

iceberg
image
incisor
infection
insect

instinct
insulate

J

jet
joint

L

larva
lava
leaf
length
lens
liquid
lungs

M

magnet
mammal
mantle
marble
marine biologist
mass
matter
melting point
membrane
mercury
meteor
meter
metric
microscope
mineral
model
moisture
molar
mold
molecule
moon
motion
muscle

N

natural resource
nerves
nucleus

O

optical
orbit
organ
organism
outlet
ovary
oxygen

P

paramecium
parasite
pendulum
periodic
pesticide
phase
physical
pitch
planet
plankton
pollen
pollute
population
power
predator
predict
prescribe
preserve
prey
produce
property
protein
protozoan
prove
pulse

pupa
pupil
pure

R

radiant
rainfall
range
rate
recycle
red blood cell
reflection
reproduction
reptile
response
retina
revolve
rib
ridge
root

S

saliva
satellite
scale
season
sediment
sedimentary
seed
senses
series
skeleton
skin
smog
solid
solution
sound
space
sperm
spinal
spore

starch

stem

stimulus

stomach

surface

survive

switch

system

T

taste

temperature

tendon

terrarium

thermometer

thunder

tides

transparent

treatment

V

variable

vein

vibration

vitamin

volcano

W

water vapor

wave

weight

Science Vocabulary—Intermediate

A

accelerate

acid

addictive

adrenal glands

alcohol

alimentary canal

alloy

alternating current

altitude

amino acid

ampere

amphetamine

anatomy

angle of incidence

angle of reflection

annual

anthropology

antibiotic

aorta

approximate

archeologist

artery

artifact

asexual

asteroid

astrology

atom

atomic

automatic

autonomic

average

B

ball-and-socket joint

barbiturates

base

biceps

bifocal

bile

binocular

biological clock

biologist

biome

biosphere

blood type

brain

bronchial tubes

C

caffeine

calculate

calorie

cancer

carbon

carbon monoxide

carcinogen

cardiac

carrier

central nervous system

cerebrum

characteristics

charge

chemotherapy

chromosome

cilia

circulatory

circumference

cirrus

classification

cocaine

cocoon

colony

color blindness

condensation

conditioned response

conservation

consumer

crystal

culture

cumulus

cycle

D

data

deaf

deficiency

demographer

deoxyribonucleic acid (DNA)

depressant

desalinization
dew point
diet
diffuse
dig
digestive tract
direct current
discharge
disinfectant
dissect
distillation
dominant trait
dormant
drug
dry-cell battery

E

earthquake
ecology
electrodes
electrolyte
electromagnetic
electron
element
elevation
ellipse
endocrine
enzyme
epidemic
epidermis
evolution
excretion
experimental
extraterrestrial
eye

F

facet
farsightedness
fault

fauna
ferment
fetus
fever
filtration
fission
flora
focal point
formula
fossil fuels
fungus
fuse
fusion

G

galaxy
galvanometer
gene
generation
generator
genetics
geologist
geothermal energy
germ
gestation
gland
glucose
granite
graph
graphite
growth

H

hallucinatory
heart
hemoglobin
hemophilia
heredity
heroin
hormone

host
humidity
hybrid
hydrocarbon
hypothesis

I

identical twins
igneous
immunity
impulse
inertia
infrared
inherit
inoculate
insoluble
interaction
intestine
intoxication
invertebrate
involuntary muscle

K

kidney
kinetic energy

L

large intestine
lifespan
limestone
ligament
liter
litmus
liver
lymph node

M

magma
magnetic field
marijuana

marine
marrow
maturity
medium
medulla
metabolism
metamorphic
metamorphosis
mitosis
mixture
morphine
moss
mutation

N

narcotic
natural selection
nearsightedness
negative
nervous system
neuron
neutral
neutron
nicotine
nitrate
nitrogen
noise
nuclear energy
nutrient
nutrition

O

observe
olfactory
opaque
orbital
ore
organic
osmosis

ossification
ovulation
oxidation
oxide
ozone

P

pancreas
pasteurization
perennial
periodic table
peripheral
petrified
pH
photosynthesis
pigment
pituitary
plasma
poliomyelitis
pollination
pollution
porous
potential energy
precipitation
primate
probability
pulley
pulmonary

Q

qualitative
quantitative
quarantine

R

reaction
recessive trait
recharge
refine
reflex
refraction
relative humidity
resistance
respiration
Rh factor
ribonucleic acid (RNA)
rickets
rod
roughage

S

saturate
scurvy
self-preservation
sensory
small intestine
smooth muscle
solar energy

solar system
species
sphere
spinal cord
static electricity
sterilization
stimulant
symbiosis
symbol
symmetry
synpase

T

taxonomy
telescope
technology
theory
thermostat
tissue
tolerance
trace elements
transfer
translucent
turbine

U

ultraviolet
universe
uvula

V

vaccination
vacuum
valve
vapor
vertebrate
vertical
virus
viscosity
vocal cords
voltage
volume
voluntary music

W

warm-blooded
water pressure
wave length
withdrawal

Y

yeast culture

Z

zoologist
zygote

A Quick Course in Computerese

accessories—mechanical components that can be added to the basic computer; also called *peripherals*.

acoustic coupler—instrument that changes the computer's code into sound waves so that information can be sent to another computer via telephone wires; a *modem*.

alphanumeric—character, either a letter or a number.

array—display of more than one sequence of letters, numerals, or other characters.

"The Reading Teacher's Book of Lists, © 1984 Prentice-Hall, Inc., Englewood Cliffs, NJ 07632. By E. Fry, J. Polk, and D. Fountoukidis."

bit—the smallest amount of information that can be known; for example, *0* or *1, plus* or *minus, on* or *off.*

branch—at a given point the computer, because of the data it has received and the program it is using, stops following a sequential order of steps, goes to another point in the program, and follows the steps there; the computer may return to the original sequence depending on the program.

bug—error.

byte—the space needed to store one character (letter, number, or symbol) of information; this is not the same as a *bit* (actually, it is equal to eight bits).

chip—small piece of material on which one to several thousand circuits have been etched.

command—direction to the computer that is acted upon as soon as it has been received.

computer—electronic device that takes in data in the form of numbers, words, or symbols, and acts or performs an operation on those data according to the directions it is given.

computer language—one of several organized sets of rules, codes, and procedural directions that is used to communicate with the computer; an example is BASIC (Beginner's All-purpose Symbolic Instruction Code).

control characters—characters or functions that can be used by holding down the key marked CTRL while pressing another key on the keyboard.

CPU (central processing unit)—the part of the computer that controls the accessories and memory.

CRT (cathode ray tube)—display screen like that of a TV.

data—information of any kind.

debugging—locating the source of an error and correcting it.

execute—do what a direction, command, or program says to do.

expression—combination of characters that can be treated or evaluated as a single quantity.

floppy disk—flexible plastic magnetic disk about the size of a 45 RPM record, which is used to store programs and data.

hardware—the basic mechanical parts of the computer, generally consisting of a keyboard (like a typewriter keyboard), a CPU, and a video display terminal or CRT.

input—data going into a computer device.

interface—connect two or more devices or components.

iterate—repeatedly carry out a set of commands or instructions; also called a *loop.*

loop—see *iterate.*

memory—the part of the computer that stores information and instructions; memory capacity is measured in *kilobytes* (how many thousands of character spaces of information it can accommodate—48K = 48,000 letters, numerals, or symbols).

menu—the list of options from which you can choose.

modem (*modulator/demodulator*)—instrument that changes the computer's binary code into sound waves so that information can be sent from one computer to another via telephone wires.

monitor—TV screen manufactured to be connected to a computer; also called a *CRT*, a *screen*, or a *video display terminal*.

output—data or information coming out of a computer.

peripherals—mechanical components that can be added to the basic computer; for example, an audiocassette recorder/player (used to enter a program into the computer or to save a program or data on the cassette tape) or a disk drive (a unit that is used like the cassette tape player to enter the program or to store information).

printer—mechanical device that prints out on paper what you see on your CRT or monitor.

program—set of directions written in a programming language, which tells the computer what to do and in what order to do it.

RAM (random access memory)—the main memory of the computer, which holds the data put into the computer by the user; they can be retrieved, added to, removed, or operated on; to save RAM data it must be sent into storage memory before you turn off the computer or it will be lost.

ROM (read only memory)—this data cannot be changed by the user of the computer; it was put into the computer by the manufacturer to establish how the computer works; for example, it is in this type of memory that the computer's language (BASIC, Pascal, etc.) is stored.

software—another word for *computer program*.

storage memory—secondary place to store quantities of data, usually on a disk or on a cassette tape.

string—sequence of letters, numerals, and/or other characters.

subroutine—portion of a program that can be called into use with a special command; it is like a program within a program.

syntax—rules for exactly how an instruction to the computer can be written in order to be understood and executed.

WORDS THAT EXPRESS FEELINGS

This is an odd category of words. They tend to view the world from the inside out. Basically, they don't describe how you look but rather how you feel or how you suppose someone else feels. They are used widely in poetry, novels, and short stories. They are useful to your students as writers and readers who wish to try to understand the human condition on an individual and intimate basis.

Reading is not all seeking information, learning factual news, following directions, or describing scientific experiments. These words open up the world of emotion and sensation. This should be part of your school and your reading lessons.

For an extension of these lists or any word in them, you will find a thesaurus very valuable. These lists give just a taste of the richness of the English language.

Emotive Words

Love—Affection—Concern

admired	considerate	good	mild	respectful
adorable	cooperative	helpful	moral	sensitive
affectionate	cordial	honest	neighborly	sweet
agreeable	courteous	honorable	nice	sympathetic
altruistic	dedicated	hospitable	obliging	tender
amiable	devoted	humane	open	thoughtful
benevolent	empathetic	interested	optimistic	tolerant
benign	fair	just	patient	trustworthy
brotherly	faithful	kind	peaceful	truthful
caring	forgiving	kindly	pleasant	understanding
charitable	friendly	lenient	polite	unselfish
comforting	generous	lovable	reasonable	warm
congenial	genuine	loving	receptive	
conscientious	giving	mellow	reliable	

Elation—Joy

amused	comical	elevated	excited	glorious	happy
blissful	contented	enchanted	fantastic	good	humorous
brilliant	delighted	enthusiastic	fit	grand	inspired
calm	ecstatic	exalted	gay	gratified	jovial
cheerful	elated	excellent	glad	great	joyful

"The Reading Teacher's Book of Lists, © 1984 Prentice-Hall, Inc., Englewood Cliffs, NJ 07632. By E. Fry, J. Polk, and D. Fountoukidis."

jubilant	marvelous	pleased	splendid	thrilled	vivacious
magnificent	overjoyed	proud	superb	tremendous	wonderful
majestic	pleasant	satisfied	terrific	triumphant	

Potency

able	competent	effective	healthy	powerful	stouthearted
adequate	confident	energetic	heroic	robust	strong
assured	courageous	fearless	important	secure	sure
authoritative	daring	firm	influential	sharp	tough
bold	determined	forceful	intense	skillful	virile
brave	durable	gallant	manly	spirited	
capable	dynamic	hardy	mighty	stable	

Depression

abandoned	dejected	downtrodden	hurt	obsolete	stranded
alien	demolished	dreadful	jilted	ostracized	tearful
alienated	depressed	estranged	kaput	overlooked	terrible
alone	desolate	excluded	loathed	pathetic	unhappy
awful	despairing	forlorn	lonely	pitiful	unloved
battered	despised	forsaken	lonesome	rebuked	whipped
blue	despondent	gloomy	lousy	regretful	worthless
burned	destroyed	glum	low	rejected	wrecked
cheapened	discarded	grim	miserable	reprimanded	
crushed	discouraged	hated	mishandled	rotten	
debased	dismal	hopeless	mistreated	ruined	
defeated	downcast	horrible	moody	rundown	
degraded	downhearted	humiliated	mournful	sad	

Distress

afflicted	disgusted	futile	nauseated	skeptical	unlucky
anguished	disliked	grief	offended	speechless	unpopular
awkward	displeased	helpless	pained	strained	unsatisfied
baffled	dissatisfied	hindered	perplexed	suspicious	unsure
bewildered	distrustful	impaired	puzzled	swamped	
clumsy	disturbed	impatient	ridiculous	tormented	
confused	doubtful	imprisoned	sickened	touchy	
constrained	foolish	lost	silly	ungainly	

"The Reading Teacher's Book of Lists, © 1984 Prentice-Hall, Inc., Englewood Cliffs, NJ 07632. By E. Fry, J. Polk, and D. Fountoukidis."

Fear—Anxiety

afraid	dreading	insecure	overwhelmed	tense
agitated	embarrassed	intimidated	panicky	terrified
alarmed	fearful	jealous	restless	timid
anxious	fidgety	jittery	scared	uncomfortable
apprehensive	frightened	jumpy	shaky	uneasy
bashful	hesitant	nervous	shy	worrying
desperate	horrified	on edge	strained	

Impotency—Inadequacy

anemic	disabled	impotent	insecure	small	unqualified
broken	exhausted	inadequate	meek	strengthless	unsound
cowardly	exposed	incapable	powerless	trivial	useless
crippled	fragile	incompetent	puny	unable	vulnerable
defective	frail	ineffective	shaken	uncertain	weak
deficient	harmless	inept	shaky	unfit	
demoralized	helpless	inferior	sickly	unimportant	

Anger—Hostility—Cruelty

agitated	blunt	cruel	hateful	mean	savage
aggravated	bullying	disagreeable	hostile	nasty	severe
aggressive	callous	enraged	impatient	obstinate	spiteful
angry	combative	envious	inconsiderate	outraged	vicious
annoyed	contrary	fierce	insensitive	perturbed	vindictive
arrogant	cool	furious	intolerant	resentful	violent
belligerent	cranky	hard	irritated	rough	wrathful
biting	cross	harsh	mad	rude	

Touch

bumpy	damp	hot	rough	silky	soft	velvety
cold	frosty	icy	sandpapery	slick	sticky	warm
cool	gooey	bumpy	sharp	smooth	stinging	wet
crisp						

Sight

blinding	colorful	dull	fuzzy	hazy	sheer	sparkling
bright	dark	fluffy	glistening	pale	shiny	swirling
brilliant	dim	foggy	glowing	shadowy		

Sound

bang	crash	hiss	rumble	splash	thump	wail
buzz	groan	hoarse	snarl	squeak	thunderous	whine
clatter	growl	moan	snort	thud	tinkle	

Taste

bitter	salty	sour	sweet	tart
peppery	savory	spicy	tangy	

Smell

acrid	choking	fragrant	mediciny	smoky
antiseptic	clean	fresh	putrid	stuffy

Hunger

bloated	famished	hungry	starved
empty	full	nauseated	stuffed

Kinesthetic (Muscle Sense)

heavy	light	shaky	tired
jerky	pain	smooth	tremble
knotted	relaxed	strong	weak

"The Reading Teacher's Book of Lists, © 1984 Prentice-Hall, Inc., Englewood Cliffs, NJ 07632. By E. Fry, J. Polk, and D. Fountoukidis."

FREQUENTLY MISSPELLED WORDS

There are many lists of so-called spelling demons, or words that give students particular trouble. The lists on the following pages are certainly not complete, but they will give you the idea of what a spelling demon list looks like. They also can be used for some tough but meaningful spelling lessons.

Many of the other lists in this book are suitable for spelling lists: the Instant Words, phonograms (they are particularly easy), and confusing words. Specialized word lists like the academic content words (mathematics, science, etc.) make interesting spelling lists for special subjects or special groups of students.

The teaching of spelling is a vast area. Spelling workbooks often have special teaching formats, such as introducing the words on Monday, writing them in sentences on Tuesday, studying their phonic elements on Wednesday, having a trial test on Thursday (so you can learn from your mistakes), and then giving the big test on Friday. You can use variations or modifications of this in teaching any list of spelling words. Teachers often have success in adding some kind of reward system, such as gold stars, bar charts of each student's test scores, prizes for the top third of the class, and so on.

In some cases, syllabication can be used successfully as one step in learning or spelling the new word. Other kinds of word elements, such as prefixes, roots, and suffixes, also can contribute to word learning. Certain words have particularly odd phoneme–grapheme correspondences, and these should be pointed out for students who benefit by a phonic or sound-spelling approach. In other situations, the whole word or root memorization approach seems to work best.

It is important for the teacher to call attention to correct spelling both in separate spelling lessons and in correcting students' writing. A valuable technique is to have each student compile his or her own spelling demon list of personal misspellings and practice on it.

Spelling Demons—197 Words Frequently Misspelled by Elementary Students

about	always	been	children	cough	decorate
address	among	before	chocolate	could	didn't
advise	April	birthday	choose	couldn't	doctor
again	arithmetic	blue	Christmas	country	does
all right	aunt	bought	close	cousin	early
along	awhile	built	color	cupboard	Easter
already	balloon	busy	come	dairy	easy
although	because	buy	coming	dear	enough

every	hello	o'clock	right	surely	until
everybody	here	off	rough	surprise	used
favorite	hospital	often	route	surrounded	vacation
February	hour	once	said	swimming	very
fierce	house	outside	Santa Claus	teacher	wear
first	instead	party	Saturday	tear	weather
football	knew	peace	says	terrible	weigh
forty	know	people	school	Thanksgiving	were
fourth	laid	piece	schoolhouse	their	we're
Friday	latter	played	several	there	when
friend	lessons	plays	shoes	they	where
fuel	letter	please	since	though	which
getting	little	poison	skiing	thought	white
goes	loose	practice	skis	through	whole
grade	loving	pretty	some	tired	women
guard		principal	something	together	would
guess	making		sometime	tomorrow	write
	many	quarter	soon	tonight	writing
half	maybe	quit	store	too	wrote
Halloween	minute	quite	straight	toys	
handkerchief	morning		studying	train	you
haven't	mother	raise	sugar	traveling	your
having		read	summer	trouble	you're
hear	name	ready	Sunday	truly	
heard	neither	receive	suppose	Tuesday	
height	nice	received	sure	two	
	none	remember			

Spelling Demons—195 Words Frequently Misspelled by Secondary Students

absence	advice	argument	calendar	conscious
acceptable	against	arrangement	category	controversial
accommodate	aisle	athlete	cemetery	controversy
accustom	amateur	bargain	certainly	council
ache	analyze	belief	cite	criticize
achievement	annually	beneficial	comparative	definitely
acquire	anticipated	benefited	concede	definition
across	apparent	breathe	conceive	descendant
adolescent	appreciate	Britain	condemn	describe
advantageous	arctic	bury	conscience	description
advertisement	arguing	business	conscientious	desert

dilemma	height	necessary	prevalent	sophomore
diligence	heroes	niece	principal	stationary
dining	hypocrite	noticeable	principle	studying
disastrous	incredible	numerous	privilege	substantial
discipline	interest		probably	subtle
disease	interrupt	occasion	procedure	succeed
dissatisfied	irrelevant	occurred	proceed	succession
	its	occurrence	profession	supersede
endeavor		occurring	professor	surprise
effect	jealousy	opinion	prominent	susceptible
embarrass	led	opportunity	pursue	technique
emigrate	leisurely			thorough
environment	license	paid	quiet	tragedy
especially	lieutenant	parallel	receipt	transferred
exaggerate	listener	paralyzed	receive	tremendous
exceed	lose	particular	recommend	
except	luxury	performance	referring	unnecessary
exercise		personal	renowned	vacuum
exhausted	magnificent	personnel	repetition	valuable
existence	maneuver	pleasant	restaurant	vegetable
experience	marriage	politician	rhythm	vengeance
explanation	mathematics	portrayed		villain
fascinate	medicine	possession	saucer	visible
formerly	mere	possible	seize	waive
	miniature	practical	sense	woman
gaiety	miscellaneous	preferred	separate	wrench
gauge	mischief	prejudice	sergeant	write
grammar	moral	prepare	shining	writing
guarantee	muscle	prescription	similar	yacht
guidance	mysterious	prestige	sincerely	

Wise Guys—Bet You Can't Spell These

Antidisestablishmentarianism: State support of the church.

Supercalifragilisticexpialidocious: Mary Poppins says it means "good."

Pneumonultramicroscopicsilicovolcanoconiosis: Lung disease caused by inhaling silica dust.

Floccinaucinihilipilification: Action of estimating as worthless.

WORDS THAT HAVE BEEN TORN APART
OR SMASHED TOGETHER

In this section are some interesting words that have obvious origins. These are words that have been shortened or clipped by common use, as in *sub* for *submarine.* Zipf's Principle is applied when common use shortens a word. It is a standard principle in linguistics.

In our blend word list, there are words like *motor* and *hotel,* which have been crunched together to form *motel.* Perhaps the ultimate crunching is just to use an acronym or the initials of the words (sometimes called initializations) to form a new word, such as *SALT* or *SCUBA* Acronyms are read as words by most people.

Contractions and compound words are two traditional ways of putting words together. You probably will find the grouping of contractions by verb interesting and a good teaching idea. It is nearly impossible to get a complete list of compound words, but ours is pretty extensive. Perhaps you and your students can come up with a few more.

These lists will help get across the idea that many words come from putting together other words or slicing off parts of longer words and phrases. This is pretty basic etymology, but it will provide some interesting insights for developing readers.

If you are having a boring day and want some pure fun, show the students some of the blend words from this list and get them to make up some of their own blend words or acronyms. *Ice cream* and *candy,* might become *iceandy.* For acronyms, and initials you already know about TGIF, but maybe you get the MMB (Monday Morning Blues).

Have some fun chopping and compressing words. These lists illustrate active linguistics principles, and they can help your students better understand the language.

Blend Words—Words That Have Been Crunched Together

autobus	automobile + omnibus	motorcade	motor + cavalcade
brunch	breakfast + lunch	smash	smack + mash
chortle	chuckle + snort	smog	smoke + fog
gerrymander	Gerry + salamander	splatter	splash + spatter
glimmer	gleam + shimmer	squiggle	squirm + wriggle
moped	motor + pedal	telethon	television + marathon
motel	motor + hotel	twirl	twist + whirl
motocross	motor + cross country		

Clipped Words—Words Shortened by Common Use

ad	advertisement	memo	memorandum
auto	automobile	mike	microphone
bike	bicycle	mod	modern
burger	hamburger	paratroops	parachute troops
bus	omnibus	pen	penitentiary
champ	champion	phone	telephone
coed	coeducational student	pike	turnpike
con	convict	plane	airplane
conman	confidence man	prom	promenade
cuke	cucumber	ref	referee
deb	debutante	skylab	sky laboratory
dorm	dormitory	sub	submarine
drape	drapery	tails	coattails
exam	examination	taxi	taxicab (taximeter
flu	influenza		cabriolet)
fridge	refrigerator	teen	teenager
gas	gasoline	tie	necktie
grad	graduate	trig	trigonometry
gym	gymnasium	tux	tuxedo
hifi	high fidelity	typo	typographical error
lab	laboratory	van	caravan
limo	limousine	vet	veteran; veterinarian
lunch	luncheon	wig	periwig
math	mathematics		

Acronyms and Initials—New Words and Terms from Initials (Also see Abbreviations in section IV.)

ACTION	American Council to Improve Our Neighborhoods
AID	Agency for International Development
AIDS	Acquired Immune Deficiency Syndrome
APO	Army Post Office
ASAP	As soon as possible
AWOL	Absent without leave
BASIC	Beginners All-purpose Symbolic Instruction Code
BASIC	British–American Scientific International Commercial English
BBC	British Broadcasting Corporation

BLT	Bacon, lettuce, and tomato
BMOC	Big man on campus
BTO	Big-time operator
CARE	Cooperative for American Relief Everywhere
CB	Citizens' Band
CETA	Comprehensive Employment and Training Act
CLASS	Computer-based Laboratory for Automated School Systems
CLASSMATE	Computer Language to Aid and Stimulate Scientific, Mathematical and Technical Education
COBOL	Common Business-Oriented Language
COD	Cash on delivery
CORE	Congress of Racial Equality
CPO	Chief petty officer
DA	District attorney
DDT	Dichlorodiphenyltrichloroethane
DEW	Distant Early Warning
DEWLINE	Distant Early Warning Line
DOA	Dead on arrival
EDP	Electronic data processing
EEG	Electroencephalogram
EKG,ECG	Electrocardiogram
ERA	Equal Rights Amendment
EURAILPASS	European railway passenger
FIAT	Fabbrica Italiana Automobili Torino
FORTRAN	Formula Translation
GASP	Group Against Smoking in Public
GESTAPO	Geheime Staats Polizei
GI	Government issue
HQ	Headquarters
HUD	Housing and Urban Development
ICBM	Intercontinental ballistic missile
IQ	Intelligence quotient
JAYCEES	U.S. Junior Chamber of Commerce
JEEP	General Purpose (vehicle)
JOBS	Job Opportunities for Better Skills
LASER	Light amplification by stimulated emission of radiation
LIFO	Last in, first out
LP	Long playing (phonograph record)
LSD	Lysergic acid diethylamide
MIA	Missing in action

"The Reading Teacher's Book of Lists, © 1984 Prentice-Hall, Inc., Englewood Cliffs, NJ 07632. By E. Fry, J. Polk, and D. Fountoukidis."

MO	Modus operandi
MYOB	Mind your own business
NAACP	National Association for the Advancement of Colored People
NABISCO	National Biscuit Company
NASA	National Aeronautics and Space Administration
NATO	North Atlantic Treaty Organization
NAZI	National Socialist German Worker's Party
NOW	National Organization for Women
OPEC	Organization of Petroleum Exporting Countries
PA	Public address
PAC	Pacific Athletic Conference
PDQ	Pretty darn quick
POW	Prisoner of war
PS	Postscript
PUSH	People United to Save Humanity
RADAR	Radio detecting and ranging
RIP	Rest in peace
ROTC	Reserve Officer Training Corps
RSVP	Répondez s'il vous plait
RV	Recreational vehicle
SALT	Strategic Arms Limitation Talks
SCUBA	Self contained underwater breathing apparatus
SNAFU	Situation normal, all fouled up
SNCC	Student Nonviolent Coordinating Committee
SONAR	Sound navigation ranging
SWAK	Sealed with a kiss
SWAT	Special weapons action team
TEFLON	Tetrafloroethylene resin
TELEX	Teletypewriter Exchange Service
TLC	Tender loving care
TNT	Trinitrotoluene
TV	Television
UFO	Unidentified flying object
UNESCO	United Nations Educational, Scientific, and Cultural Organization
UNICEF	United Nations International Children's Education Fund
VEEP	Vice-president
VIP	Very important person
VISTA	Volunteers in Service to America

WAC	Women's Army Corps
WASP	White Anglo-Saxon Protestant
WAVES	Women Accepted for Volunteer Emergency Service
WHO	World Health Organization
ZIP	Zone Improvement Plan

Contractions—Words That Substitute Part of the Word With an Apostrophe

am	us	not	will
I'm	let's	can't	I'll
		don't	you'll
are	**would, had**	isn't	she'll
you're	I'd	won't	he'll
we're	you'd	shouldn't	it'll
they're	he'd	couldn't	we'll
	she'd	wouldn't	they'll
is, has	we'd	aren't	that'll
he's	they'd	doesn't	
she's		wasn't	
it's		weren't	
what's	**have**	hasn't	
that's	I've	haven't	
who's	you've	hadn't	
there's	we've	mustn't	
here's	they've	didn't	

Compound Words—Words Glued Together to Form a New Word

afternoon	backyard	blackboard	campfire	cowboy
airconditioning	bareback	blackout	carpool	crosswalk
airline	barefoot	bloodhound	cattail	cupboard
airmail	baseball	blueprint	classmate	cupcake
airport	basketball	bookkeeper	clipboard	cutout
anchorman	bathroom	breakfast	clothesline	
anchorwoman	bedspread	broadcast	clothespin	daydream
another	billfold	bulldog	copout	daytime
applesauce	birthday	buttercup	copperhead	dishpan
ashtray	blackbird	buttermilk	copyright	doorknob

doorway	haystack	outcome	sailboat	toothbrush
downpour	headache	outfield	sandpaper	toothpick
downstairs	headlight	outfit	scarecrow	touchdown
downtown	headquarters	outlaws	screwball	tugboat
dragonfly	highchair	outstanding	screwdriver	turntable
drawbridge	highrise	overalls	shipwreck	turtleneck
drive-in	highway	overcoat	shoelace	
driveway	holdup	overlook	shortstop	undercover
dropout	homemade	overpass	sidewalk	underground
drugstore			silverware	understand
	jellyfish	pancake	skateboard	undertake
earring		paperback	skyscraper	uproot
earthquake	landlady	payoff	slipcover	uptown
eyeball	landlord	peanut	snowdrift	
	leftover	peppermint	snowfall	vineyard
ferryboat	lifeboat	pigtail	softball	volleyball
filmstrip	lifeguard	pinball	splashdown	
fireplace	lipstick	pinpoint	spotlight	washcloth
flashback	lookout	playmate	starfish	wastebasket
flashcube	loudspeaker	playpen	streetcar	watchman
flashlight		ponytail	suitcase	watercolor
folklore	midnight	popcorn	sunbeam	waterfall
football	moonship	postcard	sunflower	waterfront
frogman	moonwalk	postman	sunrise	watermelon
frostbite	motorcycle	pushover	sunset	weatherman
fruitcake			sunshine	weekend
	newsboy	quicksand	sweatshirt	whirlpool
gentleman	newscast		sweetheart	wholesale
goldenrod	newspaper	railroad		wildcat
goldfish	newsprint	railway	teacup	windmill
grasshopper	nightgown	rainbow	textbook	windpipe
	notebook	rattlesnake	thanksgiving	windshield
haircut	nutcracker	rawhide	thumbtack	wiretapping
handcuff		redwood	thunderstorm	woodland
handlebar	oatmeal	ripoff	timetable	woodpecker
hangup	offbeat	rowboat	tiptoe	wristwatch
hardware	outboard	runway	toenail	

"The Reading Teacher's Book of Lists, © 1984 Prentice-Hall, Inc., Englewood Cliffs, NJ 07632. By E. Fry, J. Polk, and D. Fountoukidis."

BUT WHAT DOES THE WORD MEAN?

These lists are different attempts to show how meaning is derived from words.

One way is to show words that mean the same or nearly the same thing (*synonyms*). Another approach is to show words with opposite meanings (*antonyms*). Dictionaries often use synonyms in their definitions. Some dictionaries also give antonyms. There are whole books of synonyms and some special reference works, like a thesaurus, which have clusters of words or phrases, all with similar meanings.

Both synonyms and antonyms are favorites of test makers. Many standardized tests use them to measure vocabulary achievement or intelligence. These words are also taught in many reading and language arts programs. Without attempting to be exhaustive, presented here are a useful list of synonyms and a useful list of antonyms. It is easy to make drills for these lists; just put one of the words on the board or a worksheet and ask the student to come up with the synonym or antonym. Answers also will generate some interesting classroom discussions.

Another favorite of test makers is *analogies*. The key here is determining the relationship between two words and then finding other pairs that have a similar relationship. The list of analogies in this section is interesting because the words are quite simple, yet there are a variety of relationships represented. Your students may be rewarded with improved performance on tests if you have given them some experience with analogies.

Similes and *metaphors* are kissing cousins. They are figures of speech stating the same idea in slightly different words. Similes always use *as* or *like* while metaphors don't use either. For example:

Simile—She is as light as a feather.

Metaphor—She's a feather.

It is important for students to understand that *she* isn't really *a feather,* that this is just a metaphor or figure of speech. Students enjoy picking out metaphors or writing metaphors and similes.

Similes and metaphors are usually highly visual or imagistic. They make writing more real or concrete. They also make it more colorful and interesting.

Idioms cannot be understood from their literal definition. For example, *break the news* really has little to do with breaking. Rather, it is used as a more colorful way of saying that someone is informing someone. Some idioms are close to slang (*blow the whistle*), but the majority are well accepted in most kinds of more formal expression. More formal language tends to use Latin- and Greek-based words instead of idioms (*hypothesize* instead of *take a guess*).

Pure idioms are usually two or three words that often can be translated into a single word and hence should be read as a word for comprehension purposes. An idiomatic expression, on the other hand, is usually an independent clause or sentence that expresses a single concept not readily apparent from the simple meanings of the individual words. *Go jump in the lake* doesn't usually have anything to do with water. Native speakers of English learn idioms just as they learn the other elements of spoken language. For reading, all you have to do is tell them to read the whole sentence or phrase before they attempt to get the meaning. However, for ESL students, idioms present extra difficulty. They often haven't had enough exposure to the new culture to know the idiom in spoken language, so it must be taught.

Teach a whole idiom just as you would teach a single vocabulary word, because that is how it must be comprehended.

All modern English words originated in another language. The study of word origins, or *etymology,* is a huge intellectual endeavor that takes bright people a lifetime to master. This list of word origins is just a start—but it is a very interesting one. If you can give the background or origin of a new word when introducing it to your class, it will help your students learn the word. You can use this list to open up the whole topic of word origins. It might get some of your students interested in studying other languages. If you have any Spanish-, Italian-, or French-speaking students in your class, they will be delighted to know that they have a jump on the rest of the class because many English words originate from Latin, which is the base of those languages.

Synonyms—Words That Mean the Same or Nearly the Same (At Least in One Context)

have, own, possess	day, date, occasion
one, single, unit	come, arrive, reach
word, term, expression	make, build, construct
all, every, entire	part, portion, piece
say, state, remark	new, fresh, recent
use, operate, employ	sound, noise, note
many, several, numerous	take, grab, seize
make, do, construct	little, small, short
like, enjoy, be fond of	work, labor, toil
time, period, season	place, put, arrange
look, glance, see	give, grant, hand over
write, record, draft	after, following, behind
people, public, individuals	name, title, designation
call, shout, summon	good, suitable, just
find, locate, retrieve	man, mankind, homo sapiens
long, lengthy, drawn-out	think, consider, believe

"The Reading Teacher's Book of Lists, © 1984 Prentice-Hall, Inc., Englewood Cliffs, NJ 07632. By E. Fry, J. Polk, and D. Fountoukidis."

great, grand, large

help, aid, assist

before, prior to, in front of

line, mark, stripe

right, correct, proper

mean, stand for, denote

old, aged, ancient

boy, lad, youth

want, desire, crave

show, demonstrate, display

form, shape, make up

end, finish, complete

large, big, enormous

turn, revolve, twist

ask, question, probe

go, leave, depart

need, require, want

different, varied, unique

move, transport, budge

try, attempt, endeavor

kind, benign, humane, picture,
   photo, painting

change, vary, alter

play, frolic, romp

point, peak, apex

page, sheet, leaf

answer, response, reply

find, locate, recover

study, consider, reflect

still, unmoving, silent

learn, acquire, understand

world, globe, earth

high, tall, lofty

near, close by, convenient

add, increase, sum

food, nourishment, edibles

below, under, beneath

country, nation, state

keep, hold, retain

start, begin, commence

city, borough, town

story, tale, account

while, during, at the same time

might, may, perhaps

close, shut, seal

seem, appear, look

hard, difficult, troublesome

open, unlock, unseal

beginning, starting, initial

group, arrange, gather

often, frequently, repeatedly

run, gallop, trot

important, needed, necessary

children, youngsters, tots

car, auto, vehicle

night, evening, dark

walk, stroll, saunter

sea, ocean, waters

grow, increase, accumulate

take, grab, steal

carry, tote, lug

state, claim, announce

stop, halt, end

idea, thought, concept

enough, sufficient, ample

eat, devour, dine

Antonyms—Words That Mean the Opposite or Nearly the Opposite (at Least in One Context)

to—from	on—off	all—none	other—same	like—dislike
in—out	with—without	there—here	many—few	more—less
that—this	his—her	him—her	then—now	go—come
he—she	one—several	up—down	make—destroy	no—yes

same—different	started—finished	get—give
boy—girl	light—dark	part—whole
following—preceding	left—right	over—under
small—large	close—open	new—old
end—begin	hard—soft	sound—silence
well—badly	life—death	take—give
even—odd	together—apart	little—big
asked—told	group—individual	work—play
move—stay	often—seldom	alive—dead
kind—cruel	child—adult	back—front
change—remain	white—black	most—least
off—on	stop—start	after—before
away—toward	allow—prohibit	something—nothing
mother—father	leave—arrive	good—bad
answer—question	problem—solution	man—woman
found—lost	friend—enemy	great—small
high—low	first—last	help—hurt
near—far	find—lose	much—little
add—subtract	long—short	right—wrong
below—above	down—up	mean—kind
never—always	day—night	old—young

Analogies—Thinking Skills or Test Items

in:out::hot:*	small:tiny::large:	three:six::four:
mother:aunt::father:	glove:hand::boot:	princess:queen::prince:
ear:hear::mouth:	swim:pool::jog:	story:song::read:
dog:barks::bird:	easy:simple::hard:	length:weight::inches:
one:two::three:	breakfast:lunch::morning:	one:three::single:
she:her::he:	blue:round::color:	blind:deaf::see:
snow:cold::sun:	meat:beef::fruit:	pen:broom::write:
finger:hand::toe:	temperature:humidity::thermometer:	wrist:hand::ankle:
brother:boy::sister:	date:calendar::time:	water:ship::air:
bear:den::bee:	cells:skin::bricks:	engine:go::brake:
girl:mother::boy:	clam:tense::smooth:	glass:break::paper:
left:right::top:	win:lose::stop:	soap:clean::mud:
car:driver::plane:	try:attempt::avoid:	book:character::recipe:
bird:sky::fish:	minute:hour::day:	silk:smooth::sandpaper:

*To interpret this notation, say, "*In* is to *out* as *hot* is to." Since the relationship here is one of opposites, the word we're looking for is *cold*.

"*The Reading Teacher's Book of Lists*, © 1984 Prentice-Hall, Inc., Englewood Cliffs, NJ 07632. By E. Fry, J. Polk, and D. Fountoukidis."

rich:wealth::sick: help:aid::gentle: sing:pleased::shout:

green:color::cinnamon: paw:dog::fin: much:little::early:

coffee:drink::hamburger: kettle:soup::griddle: penny:dollar::foot:

arrow:bow::bullet: moon:earth::earth: runner:sled::wheel:

ceiling:room::lid: tree:lumber::wheat: cabin:build::well:

page:book::Ohio: library:books::cupboard: bread:flour::butter:

Similes—Words That Describe by Comparison

as fat as a pig

as light as a feather

as cold as ice

as lovely as a rose

as green as grass

as smooth as glass

as hard as a rock

as soft as old leather

as fresh as dew

as strong as steel

as strong as an ox

as cute as a button

as cuddly as a baby

as worn as an old shoe

as dark as night

as final as death

as busy as a bee

as happy as a lark

as hungry as a bear

as sly as a fox

as sweet as honey

as quick as a wink

as quiet as a mouse

as deaf as a post

as stubborn as a mule

as dry as a bone

as soft as silk

as meek as a lamb

as thin as a rail

as blue as a mountain lake

as deep as the ocean

as quiet as an empty church

as loud as thunder

as harsh as the clang of a fire engine

as clear as day

as musical as a flute

as bright as the sun

as white as snow

as rough as sandpaper

felt like two cents

cheeks like roses

eyes like stars

laughed like a hyena

drank like a fish

spoke like an orator

walked like an elephant

waddled like a duck

worked like a horse

sparkled like diamonds

Metaphors—Words That Paint a Picture

Ann is a walking encyclopedia.

John's head is a computer.

A rocket of a man shot past me at the finish line.

The arthritic car squeaked, rattled, and moaned down the road.

"The Reading Teacher's Book of Lists," © 1984 Prentice-Hall, Inc., Englewood Cliffs, NJ 07632. By E. Fry, J. Polk, and D. Fountoukidis."

Her porcelain skin is flawless.
She's a regular adding machine.
A fossil of a man greeted us at the door.
His sandpaper hand scratched her cheek.
Skip is a clown.
Her heart is a fountain of kindness.
The mountain of paper work seemed to grow.
Carla was a mermaid slipping through the water.
His heart is an iceberg.
The army of ants attacked the fallen lollipop.
Tom is a marionette; his brother Bill works the strings.
She is the shining star in his dark dreary life.
He is a snail when it comes to getting his work done.
Mr. Mather's bark is worse than his bite.
The toddler was a clinging vine near his mother.
His books were steamships and starships taking him to new worlds.

Idioms—Common Words That Give a Whole New Meaning Together

Back: back down, back out, back up

Blow: blow a fuse, blow hot and cold, blow your own trumpet, blow out, blow over, blow the whistle, blow up

Break: break down, break in, break into, break your word, break out, break the ice, break the news, break up, break with

Bring: bring about, bring around, bring down the house, bring (something) home to one, bring in, bring off, bring on, bring one to do something, bring out, bring around, bring up

Call: call a halt, call a spade a spade, call attention to, call for, call forth, call in, call names, call on, call out, call up

Come: come about, come across, come around, come by, come clean, come down on, come in, come in for, come into, come into your own, come off, come off it, come out, come to pass, come up, come up to, come upon

Cut: cut in, cut it out, cut someone out, cut out for, cut up

Do: do away with, do for, do in, do someone proud, do out of, do up, do well (badly) by someone, do without

Eat: eat humble pie, eat crow, eat dirt, eat someone out of house and home, eat your heart out, eat your words, eat your hat, eat out of your hand, eat their heads off

Fall: fall by the wayside, fall down, fall flat, fall for, fall in with, fall off, fall out, fall over each other, fall short, fall through

"The Reading Teacher's Book of Lists," © 1984 Prentice-Hall, Inc., Englewood Cliffs, NJ 07632. By E. Fry, J. Polk, and D. Fountoukidis."

Get: get along, get at, get away with, get back at, get by, get carried away by, get even with, get in with, get into, get on, get on someone's nerves, get your back up, get someone's goat, get out of, get over, get the better of, get the hang of, get up, get wind of

Give: give a damn, give away, give in, give off, give out, give up

Go: go all out, go by, go down, go easy, go far, go for, go in for, go into, go off the deep end, go on, go one better, go out, go over, go to the dogs, go with, go with the crowd, go without

Hang: hang around, hang on, hang out, hang up

Have: have it both ways, have it coming, have it in for someone, have it out with someone

Hit: hit it off, hit your stride, hit the books, hit the ceiling, hit the roof, hit the hay, hit the sack, hit the headlines, hit the high points (spots), hit the nail on the head, hit upon

Hold: hold a candle to, hold forth, hold on, hold your own

Keep: keep a straight face, keep company, keep on, keep your head, keep your head above water, keep your temper, keep your word, keep open house, keep the pot boiling, keep the wolf from the door, keep to (a plan, a promise, your word, etc.), keep up, keep up appearances, keep up with

Knock: knock about, knock around, knock dead, knock down, knock for a loop, knock off, knock out

Lay: lay a finger on someone, lay aside, lay down one's life, lay down the law, lay hands on, lay it on, lay off, lay your hand on something, lay yourself open to, lay out, lay up

Let: let off steam, let on, let your hair down, let sleeping dogs lie, let the cat out of the bag, let up

Look: look down on, look down your nose, look for, look into, look out, look up, look up to someone

Make: make a move, make a play for, make certain, make something do, make ends meet, make fun of, make good, make haste, make head or tail of something, make it, make out, make over, make shift with, make sure, make the fur fly, make the grade, make up, make up for, make up your mind, make up to

Play: play at something, play down, play fast and loose, play havoc with, play hell, play hooky, play into someone's hands, play on, play second fiddle, play the devil, play the fool, play the game

Pull: pull a fast one, pull in your belt, pull off, pull your socks up, pull your weight, pull strings, pull through, pull to pieces, pull together, pull up, pull the wool over your eyes, pull up stakes

Put: put down, put forward, put in for, put off, put on, put your cards on the table, put your foot down, put out, put right, put two and two together, put up, put up with

Run: run across, run into, run away, run down, run foul of, run in, run out
of, run over, run ragged, run rings around, run through

See: see about, see eye to eye, see into, see through, see to

Sit: sit on, sit on the fence, sit out, sit pretty, sit tight, sit up

Take: take a back seat, take a powder, take after, take care, take it easy, take
someone or something for, take for granted, take heart, take ill, take in,
take issue, take it easy, take it from me, take it hard, take it into your
head, take it out of someone, take something lying down, take note of,
take off, take on, take your time, take out, take over, take the cake, take
to heart, take the trouble, take it upon yourself

Throw: throw a fit, throw a party, throw in the sponge, throw light on,
throw off, throw one's weight around, throw out, throw up

Turn: turn a cold shoulder to, turn a deaf ear, turn down, turn in, turn loose,
turn on, turn your head, turn out, turn over (money), turn over a new
leaf, turn the tables on someone, turn to, turn turtle, turn up

Idiomatic Expressions—Don't Take Everything Literally!

Take the tiger by the tail.

I got it straight from the horse's mouth.

We're in hot water.

Drop me a line.

I'll do it when the cows come home.

Go fly a kite.

That's a sharp tie.

I'd really like to catch her eye.

We have to straighten up the house.

Go jump in the lake.

Button your lip.

Can you dig it?

Cat got your tongue?

You're off your rocker.

Get out of my hair.

Time flies.

You're out of sight.

He has a green thumb.

Keep a stiff upper lip.

Lend a hand.

She let the cat out of the bag.

Cut it out.

She gave him a dirty look.

The traffic was heavy.

We don't see eye to eye on this.

Stop pulling my leg.

It looks like a record snow.

It's raining cats and dogs.

It's a dog's life.

We're all in the same boat.

You'll catch a cold that way.

He's a cracker-jack mechanic.

The boss just gave him the ax.

You could have knocked me over with a feather.

By the skin of your teeth you won the game.

Tom caught the train at eight.

You really put your foot in your mouth this time.

Expensive? Naw, it's just chicken feed.

Get off my back!

She's always a ball of fire.

The criminal tried to beat the rap.

The manager's over a barrel on this one.

Somebody might blow the whistle on your plan.

We're up a creek.

Stop bugging me!

The boys had a bull session Friday night.

You've hit it on the button.

The judge threw the book at him.

This car can stop on a dime.

I'll put this one in the circular file.

The boys were just shooting the breeze.

He quit cold turkey.

The way he got the job was dirty pool.

That's the way the cookie crumbles.

He's out on his ear.

She's over the hill.

He got in by the seat of his pants.

I'm hung up on this problem.

He's out in left field.

I gave up the rat race.

He's got rocks in his head.

It's in the bag.

Word Origins—Some Interesting Words and Their Origins

albino—Latin (*albus*), white   alligator—Spanish (*el lagarto*), great lizard
amp—named after André Ampere for his work in electricity

"The Reading Teacher's Book of Lists, © 1984 Prentice-Hall, Inc., Englewood Cliffs, NJ 07632. By E. Fry, J. Polk, and D. Fountoukidis."

April—named for the Greek goddess Aphrodite, the goddess of love

astrology—Greek (*astron logos*), discussion of stars

audio—Latin (*audire*), hear

August—named for the emperor Augustus Caesar

bacteria—Greek (*bakterion*), little rods

barbecue—Caribbean Indian (*barbacoa*), frame of sticks

barber—Latin (*barba*), beard

bicycle—Greek (*bi kyklos*), two circles

binoculars—Latin (*bini oculus*), two eyes at a time

bloomers—named for Amelia Bloomer, who made them fashionable

bonus—Latin (*bonus*), good

bowie knife—named for James Bowie, the frontiersman who invented it

boycott—named for Captain Charles Boycott, with whom a group of Irish farmers and tenants refused to deal

Braille—named for Louis Braille, who invented this coding for the blind

Bunsen burner—named for Robert Bunsen, who invented it

capital—Latin (*caput*), head

chauvinist—named for Nicholas Chauvin, who worshipped Napoleon and France uncritically

chop suey—Chinese (*tsap sui*), odds and ends

collage—Greek (*kolla*), glue

czar—Latin (*Caesar*), emperor

democracy—Greek (*demos kratos*), rule of the people

dessert—French (*desservir*), clear away the table

dictate—Latin (*dicere*), say

diesel—named for Rudolf Diesel, who invented this type of engine

dinosaur—Greek (*deinos sauros*), terrible lizard

dodo—Portuguese (*doudo*), fool

drama—Greek (*drama*), deed or play

dunce—named for Johannes Duns Scotus, a theologian whose followers were called Dunsmen

enormous—Latin (*ex norma*), out of the usual pattern

equation—Latin (*aequus*), even or just

fable—Latin (*fari*), speak about

fervor—Latin (*fervere*), boil or glow

foreign—Latin (*foras*), outside

fossil—Latin (*fodere*), dig

gelatin—Latin (*gelare*), freeze

Graham cracker—named for Sylvester Graham, a vegetarian

guillotine—named for Dr. Joseph Guillotin, who invented it during the French Revolution hydrant—Greek (*hydor*), water

iceberg—Dutch (*ijsberg*), ice mountain

iodine—Greek (*ion eidos*), violet form

January—named for the Roman god Janus

July—named for the Roman emperor Julius Caesar

kaleidoscope—Greek (*kalos eidow skopein*), look at pretty forms

kindergarten—German (*kinder garten*), garden of children

lunatic—Latin (*luna*), moonstruck

magazine—Arabic (*makhazin*), storehouse

manual—Latin (*manus*), hand

March—named for the Roman god Mars, the god of war

mesa—Spanish (*mesa*), table

monarch—Greek (*monos archein*), rule alone

noun—Latin (*nomen*), name

ode—Greek (*oide*), song

orange—Persian (*narang*), fragrant

platypus—Greek (*platys pous*), flat-footed

point—Latin (*pungere*), pierce

polygon—Greek (*polys gonia*), having many angles

potpourri—French (*pot pourri*), rotten pot

puzzle—Middle English (*poselen*), confuse or bewilder

reptile—Latin (*repere*), crawl

rhinoceros—Greek (*rhinos keras*), horn nose

robot—Czechoslovakian (*robotnik*), slave

rupture—Latin (*rumpere*), break

sandwich—named for the fourth Earl of Sandwich, who invented it so he
    could continue to gamble without stopping for a regular meal

savvy—Latin (*sapere*), be wise

segregate—Latin (*se gregem*), apart from the herd

senate—Latin (*senex*), old man

shampoo—Hindu (*champo*), press, knead, or squeeze

shamrock—Gaelic (*seamrog*), little clover

sinister—Latin (*sinister*), left side

slogan—Gaelic (*sluagh ghairm*), army yell

society—Latin (*sicius*), companion

stein—German (*steingut*), stoneware

stirrup—Old English (*stigrap*), climbing rope

teddy bear—named for Teddy Roosevelt, who spared the life of a bear cub on
    a hunting trip in Mississippi

tentacles—Latin (*tenere*), hold

Thursday—named for the Scandinavian god Thor

tulip—Persian (*dulband*), turban
tyrannosaurus—Greek (*tyrannos sauros*), tyrant lizard
umbrella—Italian (*ombra*), shade
undulate—Latin (*unda*), wave
unit—Latin (*unus*), one
waffle—Dutch (*wafel*), wafer
werewolf—Old English (*wer wulf*), wolf man
zeppelin—named for Count Ferdinand von Zeppelin, who invented the airship

SOME STRANGE WORDS

A *palindrome* is a word or sentence that reads the same way forward and backward. They are enjoyed by people of all ages who like to have some fun with words. Here is a starter list. Get your students to find some more. The easiest to find are CVC (constant–vowel–consonant) trigrams like *dam—mad*, but there are plenty of other kinds. This might drive your brighter students slightly insane for a couple of days.

Incidentally, many decades ago a physician named Samual Orton coined the term *strepholsymbolia* to describe the pathological error of reading or writing words backward, like *saw* for *was*; however, now such reversals are usually considered just a sign of immature literacy. You can witness the phenomenon in any first grade class.

Onomatopoeic words are supposed to sound like the real sound they refer to. For example, a cow *moos*. These words are favorites with poets and comic strip writers. Entertainers love them, and children's authors use them regularly. Your students will like them and probably can add some to this list.

Palindromes—Words and Sentences That Read the Same Backward and Forward

Word Palindromes

Mom	noon	deed	did	Anna	tot
Dad	level	peep	eve	radar	dud
pop	Otto	ere	Bob	madam	toot

Sentence Palindromes

Name no one man.

Step on no pets.

Never odd or even.

Able was I ere I saw Elba.

May a moody baby doom a yam?

Madam I'm Adam.

A man, a plan, a canal, Panama!

Words That Read Differently Backwards and Forwards

Similar to palindromes are words that give different words when read backward. These words are often used in forming palindromes

but	tub	now	won	top	pot	step	pets
no	on	net	ten	stop	pots	reward	drawer
not	ton	draw	ward	sleep	peels	cod	doc

"The Reading Teacher's Book of Lists, © 1984 Prentice-Hall, Inc., Englewood Cliffs, NJ 07632. By E. Fry, J. Polk, and D. Fountoukidis."

saw	was	reed	deer	sinned	Dennis	emit	time
yam	may	leg	gel	stab	bats	sloop	pools
mood	doom	sleek	keels	star	rats	slap	pals
live	evil	strap	parts	spat	taps	keep	peek
Noel	Leon	tar	rat	span	naps		

Onomatopoeic Words—Words That Sound Like Their Meanings

bang	clatter	flippity flop	murmur	rustle	squish
beep	clink	grind	ping	slurp	thump
bong	crack	hiss	plop	smack	twang
buzz	crash	honk	quack	smash	wack
chirp	crunch	hum	rip	splash	zip
clang	ding dong	moo	roar	squeal	

II
PHONICS

WORD FAMILIES

A *phonogram* is a reading teacher's term for a cluster of letters that is only part of a word or part of a syllable but has a stable pronunciation. To make a whole word, a consonant sound or consonant blend is usually added.

The most common type of phonogram, and the type used in this list, has the beginning consonant sound or sounds missing. One value of this list is that all of the common words using each phonogram are supplied. The word list for each phonogram is sometimes called a *word family*. It is interesting to note that not all possible consonants can be placed in front of any particular phonogram.

The word families used here are fairly extensive, but we intentionally have omitted rare words and most slang words.

The World's Greatest List of Major Phonograms contains all of the phonograms that have ten or more words in their families. The World's Greatest List of Minor Phonograms contains words with less than ten words in their families. However, some of the minor phonograms, like *-ome* as in *come* and *some,* contain very common and easy words. There just are not a lot of words in the *-ome* family.

We are calling these the world's greatest lists because we have never seen such a complete list of phonograms and word families before. Many reading textbooks as well as many basal readers and workbooks contain some phonograms. We looked at a number of these sources but found no extensive lists. So we combined everything we could find· from existing texts. Then, by a stroke of good luck, we found that a rhyming dictionary was a valuable cross-reference.

Phonograms and word families are taught in many ways. Here are but a few:

1. *Word wheels* have an outer ring that contains the consonant sound and an inner ring that contains the phonogram—the students match to form words.

2. *Slip charts* work much the same way—slide a strip of paper containing the consonant sound past a fixed slot that has a phonogram next to it.

3. *Spelling lessons* are an easy way to teach word families. For example, tell your students they will have a spelling test tomorrow on 20 words. They groan. You give them the *-ack* family: *back, Jack, hack,* and so on.

4. *Workbook pages* let students fill in the missing consonant, fill in the missing phonogram, select the words with the same ending sound, and draw lines from column A of consonants to column B of phonograms to form words.

See the games mentioned in section VI.

"*The Reading Teacher's Book of Lists,* © 1984 Prentice-Hall, Inc., Englewood Cliffs, NJ 07632. By E. Fry, J. Polk, and D. Fountoukidis."

World's Greatest List of Major Phonograms

-ab (ă)
cab
gab
jab
tab
crab
drab
grab
scab
slab
stab

-ace (ā)
face
lace
mace
pace
race
brace
grace
place
space
trace

-ack (ă)
back
hack
Jack
lack
Mack
pack
quack
rack
sack
tack
black
clack
crack
knack

shack
smack
snack
stack
track
whack

-ad (ă)
bad
dad
fad
had
lad
mad
pad
sad
tad
Brad
Chad
clad
glad
shad

-ade (ā)
bade
fade
jade
made
wade
blade
glade
grade
shade
spade
trade

-ag (ă)
bag
gag

hag
lag
nag
rag
sag
tag
wag
brag
crag
drag
flag
shag
slag
snag
stag
swag

-ail (ā)
bail
fail
Gail
hail
jail
mail
nail
pail
quail
rail
sail
tail
wail
frail
snail
trail

-ain (ā)
gain
lain
main

pain
rain
vain
brain
chain
drain
grain
plain
slain
Spain
sprain
stain
strain
train

-ake (ā)
bake
cake
fake
Jake
lake
make
quake
rake
sake
take
wake
brake
drake
flake
shake
snake
stake

-all (ô)
ball
call
fall
gall

hall
mall
tall
wall
small
squall
stall

-am (ă)
dam
ham
jam
Pam
ram
Sam
yam
clam
cram
dram
gram
sham
slam
tram

-ame (ā)
came
dame
fame
game
lame
name
same
tame
blame
flame
frame
shame

-amp (ă)
camp
damp

lamp
ramp
tamp
vamp
champ
clamp
cramp
gramp
scamp
stamp
tramp

-an (ă)
ban
can
Dan
fan
man
pan
ran
tan
van
bran
clan
flan
plan
scan
span
than

-and (ă)
band
hand
land
sand
bland
brand
gland

grand
stand
strand

-ane (ā)
cane
Jane
lane
mane
pane
sane
vane
wane
crane
plane

-ang (ă)
bang
fang
gang
hang
pang
rang
sang
tang
clang
slang
sprang

-ank (ă)
bank
dank
hank
lank
rank
sank
tank
yank
blank

	-are (ã)	crash	skate	pay	-eam (ē)	-ed (ĕ)
clank		flash	state	ray	beam	bed
crank	bare	slash		say	ream	fed
drank	care	smash	-ave (ā)	way	seam	led
flank	dare	stash	cave	bray	team	Ned
Frank	fare	trash	Dave	clay	cream	red
plank	mare	thrash	gave	cray	dream	Ted
prank	rare		pave	fray	gleam	wed
shank	blare	-at (ă)	rave	gray	scream	bled
spank	flare	bat	save	play	steam	bred
stank	glare	cat	wave	pray	stream	fled
thank	scare	fat	brave	slay		Fred
-ap (ă)	share	hat	crave	spray	-ear (ē)	shed
cap	snare	mat	grave	stay	dear	shred
gap	spare	gnat	shave	stray	fear	sled
lap	square	pat	slave	tray	gear	sped
map	stare	rat			hear	
nap	-ark (ä)	sat	-aw (ô)	-eak (ē)	near	-eed (ē)
rap	bark	tat	caw	beak	rear	deed
sap	dark	vat	jaw	leak	sear	feed
tap	hark	brat	law	peak	tear	heed
chap	lark	chat	gnaw	teak	year	need
clap	mark	drat	paw	weak	clear	reed
flap	park	flat	raw	bleak	shear	seed
scrap	Clark	scat	saw	creak	smear	weed
slap	shark	slat	claw	sneak	spear	bleed
snap	spark	spat	craw	speak		breed
strap	stark	that	draw	squeak	-eat (ē)	creed
trap			flaw	streak	beat	freed
wrap	-ash (ă)	-ate (ā)	slaw		feat	greed
-ar (ä)	bash	date	squaw	-eal (ē)	heat	speed
bar	cash	fate	straw	deal	meat	steed
car	dash	gate		heal	neat	treed
far	gash	hate	-ay (ā)	meal	peat	
jar	hash	Kate	bay	peal	seat	-eep (ē)
mar	lash	late	day	real	bleat	deep
tar	mash	mate	gay	seal	cheat	jeep
char	rash	rate	hay	veal	cleat	keep
scar	sash	crate	jay	zeal	pleat	peep
spar	brash	grate	lay	squeal	treat	seep
star	clash	plate	may	steal	wheat	weep

"The Reading Teacher's Book of Lists, © 1984 Prentice-Hall, Inc., Englewood Cliffs, NJ 07632. By E. Fry, J. Polk, and D. Fountoukidis."

				-id (ĭ)	-ight (ī)	-im (ĭ)
cheep	hen	guest	drew		fight	
creep	Ken	jest	flew	bid	knight	dim
sheep	men	lest	screw	did	light	him
sleep	pen	nest	skew	hid	might	Kim
steep	wren	pest	slew	kid	night	Jim
sweep	ten	rest	stew	lid	right	rim
	yen	test	strew	quid	sight	Tim
-eet (ē)	then	vest	threw	rid	tight	vim
beet	when	west		grid	blight	brim
feet		zest	**-ice (ī)**	skid	bright	grim
meet	**-end (ĕ)**	blest	dice	slid	flight	prim
fleet	bend	chest	lice		fright	slim
greet	end	crest	mice	**-ide (ī)**	plight	swim
sheet	fend	quest	nice		slight	trim
sleet	lend		rice	bide		whim
street	mend	**-et (ĕ)**	vice	hide	**-ill (ĭ)**	
sweet	rend	bet	price	ride	bill	**-ime (ī)**
tweet	send	get	slice	side	dill	dime
	tend	jet	spice	tide	fill	lime
-ell (ĕ)	vend	let	splice	wide	gill	mime
bell	blend	met	thrice	bride	hill	time
cell	spend	net	twice	chide	ill	chime
dell	trend	pet		glide	Jill	clime
fell		set	**-ick (ĭ)**	pride	kill	crime
hell	**-ent (ĕ)**	wet	Dick	slide	mill	grime
jell	bent	yet	kick	snide	pill	prime
Nell	cent	Chet	lick	stride	quill	slime
sell	dent	fret	Nick		rill	
tell	gent	whet	pick	**-ig (ĭ)**	sill	**-in (ĭ)**
well	Kent		quick	big	till	bin
yell	lent	**-ew (ü)**	Rick	dig	will	din
dwell	rent	dew	sick	fig	chill	fin
quell	sent	few	tick	gig	drill	gin
shell	tent	hew	wick	jig	frill	kin
smell	vent	Jew	brick	pig	grill	pin
spell	went	knew	chick	rig	skill	sin
swell	scent	pew	click	wig	spill	tin
	spent	blew	flick	brig	still	win
-en (ĕ)		brew	slick	sprig	thrill	chin
Ben	**-est (ĕ)**	chew	stick	swig	trill	grin
den	best	crew	thick	twig	twill	shin
			trick			

		-ip (ĭ)	**-ive (ī)**	smock	spoke	**-op (ŏ)**
skin	zing	dip	dive	stock	stoke	bop
spin	bring	hip	five		stroke	cop
thin	cling	lip	hive	**-od (ŏ)**		hop
twin	fling	nip	jive		**-old (ō)**	mop
	sling	quip	live	cod		pop
-ind (ī)	spring	rip	chive	God	bold	sop
bind	sting	sip	drive	mod	cold	top
find	string	tip	strive	nod	fold	chop
hind	swing	zip	thrive	pod	gold	crop
kind	thing	blip		rod	hold	drop
mind	wring	chip	**-ob (ŏ)**	sod	mold	flop
rind		clip	Bob	Tod	old	plop
wind	**-ink (ĭ)**	drip	cob	clod	sold	prop
blind	kink	flip	fob	plod	told	shop
grind	link	grip	gob	prod	scold	slop
	mink	ship	job	shod		stop
-ine (ī)	pink	skip	lob	trod	**-one (ō)**	
dine	rink	slip	mob		bone	**-ope (ō)**
fine	sink	snip	knob	**-og (ŏ or ô)**	cone	cope
line	wink	strip	rob	bog	hone	dope
mine	blink	trip	sob	cog	lone	hope
nine	brink	whip	blob	fog	tone	lope
pine	chink		slob	hog	zone	mope
tine	clink	**-it (ĭ)**	snob	jog	clone	nope
vine	drink	bit		log	crone	pope
wine	shrink	fit	**-ock (ŏ)**	tog	drone	rope
brine	stink	hit	dock	clog	phone	grope
shine	think	kit	hock	flog	prone	scope
shrine		lit	lock	frog	stone	slope
spine	**-int (ĭ)**	knit	mock	grog		
swine	hint	pit	knock	slog	**-ong (ŏ)**	**-ore (ô)**
whine	lint	quit	rock	smog	bong	
	mint	sit	sock		dong	bore
-ing (ĭ)	tint	wit	tock	**-oke (ō)**	gong	core
bing	flint	flit	block	coke	long	fore
ding	glint	grit	clock	joke	song	gore
king	print	skit	crock	poke	tong	more
ping	splint	slit	flock	woke	prong	pore
ring	sprint	spit	frock	broke	strong	sore
sing	squint	split	shock	choke	thong	tore
wing	stint	twit		smoke	wrong	

wore	how	**-uck (ŭ)**	plug	**-un (ŭ)**	slunk
chore	now	buck	shrug	bun	spunk
score	row	duck	slug	fun	stunk
shore	sow	huck	smug	gun	thunk
spore	vow	luck	snug	nun	trunk
store	brow	muck	thug	pun	
swore	chow	puck		run	**-ush (ŭ)**
-orn (ô)	plow	suck	**-um (ŭ)**	sun	gush
born	prow	tuck	bum	shun	hush
corn	scow	Chuck	gum	spun	lush
horn		cluck	hum	stun	mush
morn	**-ow (ō)**	pluck	mum		rush
torn	know	shuck	rum	**-ung (ŭ)**	blush
worn	low	stuck	sum	hung	brush
scorn	row	struck	yum	lung	crush
shorn	tow	truck	chum	rung	flush
sworn	blow		drum	sung	plush
thorn	flow	**-uff (ŭ)**	glum	clung	slush
	glow	buff	plum	flung	thrush
-ot (ŏ)	show	cuff	scum	slung	
cot	slow	muff	slum	sprung	**-ut (ŭ)**
got	snow	puff	strum	stung	but
hot	stow	bluff	swum	strung	cut
jot		fluff		swung	gut
knot	**-ub (ŭ)**	gruff	**-ump (ŭ)**	wrung	hut
lot	bub	scuff	bump		jut
not	cub	snuff	dump	**-unk (ŭ)**	nut
pot	dub	stuff	hump	bunk	rut
rot	hub		jump	dunk	Tut
tot	nub	**-ug (ŭ)**	lump	funk	glut
blot	pub	bug	pump	hunk	shut
clot	rub	dug	rump	junk	slut
plot	sub	hug	sump	punk	smut
shot	tub	jug	chump	sunk	strut
slot	club	lug	clump	chunk	
spot	flub	mug	frump	drunk	
trot	grub	pug	grump	flunk	**-y (ī)**
	scrub	rug	plump	plunk	by
-ow (ou)	shrub	tug	slump	shrunk	my
bow	snub	chug	stump	skunk	cry
cow	stub	drug	trump		

dry	fry	pry	sky	spy
fly	ply	shy	sly	try

World's Greatest List of Minor Phonograms

-act (ă)	flair	-ape (ā)	-art (ä)	-ast (ă)	-ax (ă)	-eap (ē)
fact	stair	cape	cart	cast	lax	heap
pact		gape	dart	fast	max	leap
tact	-aise (ā)	nape	mart	last	tax	reap
tract	raise	rape	part	mast	wax	cheap
	praise	tape	tart	past	flax	
-aft (ă)		grape	chart	vast		-ee (ē)
raft	-ait (ā)	scrape	smart	blast	-aze (ā)	bee
craft	bait	shape	start		faze	fee
draft	gait			-atch (ă)	haze	knee
graft	trait	-ard (ä)	-ase (ā)	batch	blaze	see
shaft		bard	base	catch	craze	tee
	-alk (ô)	card	case	hatch		wee
-age (ā)	balk	guard	vase	match	-ead (ĕ)	flee
cage	talk	hard	chase	scratch	dead	glee
page	walk	lard		thatch	head	
rage	chalk	yard	-ask (ă)		lead	eek (ē)
sage	stalk		ask	-aught (ô)	read	leek
wage		-arm (ä)	cask	caught	bread	meek
stage	-ance (ă)	farm	mask	taught	dread	peek
	dance	harm	task	naught	spread	seek
-aid (ā)	lance	charm	flask	fraught	thread	week
laid	chance				tread	cheek
maid	France	-arn (ä)	-ass (ă)	-awn (ô)		creek
paid	glance	barn	bass	dawn	-ean (ē)	Greek
raid	prance	darn	lass	fawn	bean	sleek
braid	stance	yarn	mass	lawn	dean	
staid	trance		pass	pawn	Jean	-eel (ē)
		-arp (ä)	brass	yawn	lean	feel
-air (ă)	-ant (ă)	carp	class	drawn	mean	heel
fair	can't	harp	glass	prawn	wean	keel
hair	pant	tarp	grass	spawn	clean	kneel
lair	rant	sharp			glean	peel
pair	grant					reel
chair	plant					creel
	scant					steel
	slant					wheel

-eem (ē)

deem
seem
teem

-een (ē)

queen
seen
teen
green
screen
sheen

-eer (ē)

beer
deer
jeer
peer
queer
sneer
steer

-ess (ĕ)

Bess
guess
less
mess
bless
chess
dress
press
stress

-eigh (ā)

neigh
weigh
sleigh

-eight (ā)

eight
weight
freight

-ib (ĭ)

bib
fib
rib
crib

-ibe (ī)

jibe
bribe
tribe
scribe

-ie (ī)

die
fie
lie
pie
tie
vie

-ief (ē)

brief
chief
grief
thief

-ife (ī)

fife
life
wife
knife
strife

-iff (ĭ)

cliff
skiff
sniff
stiff

-ift (ĭ)

gift
lift
rift
drift
shift
swift
thrift

-ike (ī)

bike
dike
hike
like
Mike
pike
spike
strike

-ile (ī)

bile
mile
Nile
pile
tile
vile
smile
while

-ilt (ĭ)

jilt
kilt
nilt

quilt
tilt
wilt

-ince (ĭ)

mince
since
wince
prince

-ipe (ī)

pipe
ripe
wipe
gripe
snipe
stripe
tripe

-ire (ī)

fire
hire
tire
wire
spire

-irt (ŭ)

dirt
flirt
shirt
skirt
squirt

-ise (ī)

guise
rise
wise

-ish (ĭ)

dish
fish
wish
swish

-isk (ĭ)

disk
risk
brisk
frisk
whisk

-iss (ĭ)

hiss
kiss
miss
bliss
Swiss

-ist (ĭ)

list
mist
wrist
grist
twist

-itch (ĭ)

bitch
ditch
pitch
witch
switch

-ite (ī)

bite
kite
mite
quite

rite
site
white
write
spite

-ix (ĭ)

fix
mix
six

-o (ü)

do
to
who

-o (ō)

go
no
so
pro

-oach (ō)

coach
poach
roach

-oad (ō)

load
road
toad

-oak (ō)

soak
cloak
croak

-oal (ō)

coal
foal
goal
shoal

-oam (ō)

foam
loam
roam

-oan (ō)

Joan
loan
moan
groan

-oar (ô)

boar
roar
soar

-oast (ō)

boast
coast
roast
toast

-oat (ō)

boat
coat
goat
moat
bloat
float
throat

-obe (ō)

lobe
robe
globe
probe

-ode (ō)

code
lode
mode

node
rode
strode

-oil (oy)

boil
coil
foil
soil
toil
spoil

-oin (oy)

coin
join
loin
groin

-ole (ō)

dole
hole
mole
pole
role
stole
whole

-oll (ō)

poll
roll
toll
scroll
stroll
troll

-olt (ō)

bolt
colt
jolt
molt
volt

-ome (ŏ)

dome
home
Nome
Rome
tome
chrome

-ome (ŏ)

come
some

-oo (ü)

coo
goo
moo
poo
too
woo
zoo
shoo

-ood (u̇)

good
hood
wood
stood

-ood (ü)

food
mood
brood

-ook (u̇)

book
cook
hook
look
took
brook

crook
shook

-ool (ü)

cool
fool
pool
drool
school
spool
stool

-oom (ü)

boom
doom
loom
room
bloom
broom
gloom
groom

-oon (ü)

coon
loon
moon
noon
soon
croon
spoon
swoon

-oop (ü)

hoop
loop
droop
scoop
sloop
snoop
swoop
troop

-oot (ü)

boot
loot
moot
root
toot
shoot

-orch (ô)

porch
torch
scorch

-ork (ô)

cork
fork
York
stork

-ort (ô)

fort
Mort
port
short
snort
sport

-ose (ō)

hose
nose
pose
rose
chose
close
prose
those

-oss (ŏ)

boss
loss
moss

toss
cross
gloss

-ost (ŏ or ô)

cost
lost
frost

-ost (ō)

host
most
post

-otch (ŏ)

notch
blotch
crotch
Scotch

-ote (ō)

note
quote
rote
vote
wrote

-ought (ô)

bought
fought
ought
sought
brought
thought

-ough (ŭ)

rough
tough
enough
slough

-ould (u̇)

could
would
should

-ounce (ou)

bounce
pounce
flounce
trounce

-ound (ou)

bound
found
hound
mound
pound
round
sound
ground

-ouse (ou)

douse
house
mouse
souse
grouse

-out (ou)

bout
pout
scout
shout

spout
sprout
stout
trout

-outh (ou)

mouth
south
drouth

-ove (ō)

cove
clove
drove
grove

-ove (ŭ)

dove
love
glove
shove

-owl (ou)

fowl
howl
jowl
growl
prowl
scowl

-own (ou)

down
gown

town
brown
clown
crown
drown
frown

-own (ō)

known
blown
flown
grown

-oy (oi)

boy
coy
joy
Roy
soy
toy

-ud (ŭ)

bud
dud
mud
spud
stud
thud

-ude (ü)

dude
nude

rude
crude
prude

-udge (ŭ)

fudge
judge
nudge
grudge
sludge

-ue (ü)

due
Sue
blue
clue
flue
glue

-ull (ŭ)

dull
gull
hull
lull
mull

-umb (ŭ)

dumb
numb
crumb
plumb
thumb

-unch (ŭ)

bunch
hunch
lunch
munch
punch
crunch

-une (ü)

June
tune
prune

-unt (ŭ)

bunt
hunt
punt
runt
blunt
grunt
stunt

-ur (ėr)

cur
fur
blur
slur
spur

-urn (ėr)

burn
turn
churn
spurn

-urse (ėr)

curse
nurse
purse

-us (ŭ)

bus
pus
plus
thus

-ust (ŭ)

bust
dust
just
lust
rust
thrust
trust

-ute (ü)

jute
lute
flute

IRREGULAR WORDS

The words in the following list have two special characteristics: they are among the most frequently used words in our language, and they do not follow regular phonics (letter–sound) rules. For these reasons it is essential that they be taught as sight words to your young students.

A number of appealing "whole word" activities can be used. Here are three to get you started: 1. Use the words to make a word bingo game. 2. Make a relay race board game. Roll the die, land on the word, pronounce it and stay, or miss it and go back; first to the finish line wins. 3. Go fishing. Write words on paper fish, put a clip on each, drop in a pail, fish with a magnet on a string, keeping only those fish you can read.

Irregular Words—Words That Are Phonic Misfits

a	door	have	often	something	watch
again	earth	heard	old	sure	water
answer	enough	kind	on	the	were
any	example	knew	once	their	what
are	eyes	learn	one	there	where
become	father	live	only	they	who
been	few	many	other	thought	words
both	find	measure		through	work
color	four	most	people	to	world
come	friends	mother	picture	today	would
could	from	mountain	piece	two	
country	give	move	said	usually	you
do	great	of	should	want	young
does	group	off	some	was	your

LIST OF EXAMPLE WORDS

This phonics list of example words can be very useful to teachers for all kinds of reading and spelling lessons. It should enable you to quickly find 30 to 40 common examples for most graphemes and blends.

It is arranged alphabetically by *grapheme* or beginning consonant blend. A grapheme is a letter or two letters that stand for a single *phoneme* or sound. For example, *T* is the grapheme that stands for the *t* phoneme at the beginning of the word *top*, *CH* is the grapheme that stands for the phoneme at the beginning of the word *chair*. Blends are technically different in that they are usually two letters that stand for two phonemes. For example, *ST* stands for the *s* and *t* sounds that are blended together at the beginning of the word *stop*. Many phonics teaching materials teach blends as a phonics unit.

This phonics word list is further organized so that common example words are arranged with the grapheme being taught occurring in the beginning, middle, and end of a word. Of course, some graphemes and blends simply are not commonly used at the beginning or the end of a word. For example, *AY*, which makes the long *a* sound, is never found at the beginning of a word; and *BR* is never found at the end of a word.

Not all of the example words are of equal difficulty. For example, words that begin with *q* are more rare and difficult than words that begin with *t*. And even within lists, some positions are more common. For example, the final position for *AR* has easier examples than initial position examples. In other words, *bar* and *far* are easier than *arctic* and *argument*. The teacher of young children or beginning reading adults might wish to skip the more difficult example words.

Words to Illustrate 99 Phoneme–Grapheme Correspondences*

A Vowel Sound: Short (apple)

(initial)			(medial)		
and	add	am	that	has	began
at	act	animal	can	than	stand
as	adjective	ant	had	man	black
after	answer	ax	back	hand	happen
an	ask	Africa	last	plant	fast

---

*Fry, Edward, *99 Phonics Charts*. 1971. (Highland Park, NJ: Dreier Educational Systems. Now available from Jamestown Publications, Providence, RI.)

A Vowel Sound: Long Open Syllable Rule (table)

(initial)   (medial)

(initial)	(medial)			
able	paper	lazy	label	vibration
acre	lady	flavor	equator	basis
agent	baby	tomato	relation	hazy
apron	radio	navy	vapor	potato
Asia	crazy	station	enable	ladle
apex	labor	basic	volcano	vacation
April				

A—E Vowel Sound: Long Final E Rule (cake)

(initial)   (medial)

(initial)		(medial)			
ate	ape	make	late	table	baseball
able	ace	made	tale	gave	spaceship
acre		face	place	base	tablecloth
age		same	name	plane	racetrack
ache		came	wave	game	shapeless
ale		state	space	shape	

AI Vowel Sound: Long A (nail)

(initial)   (medial)

(initial)	(medial)				
aim	rain	mail	claim	obtain	faint
aid	train	pain	detail	paid	grain
ailment	wait	sail	explain	remain	rail
ail	tail	strait	fail	wait	
	chain	afraid	gain	plain	
	jail	brain	main	laid	

AY Vowel Sound: Long A (hay)

(medial)   (final)

(medial)			(final)		
always	gayly	jaywalk	day	pay	repay
mayor	haystack	player	say	gray	anyway
layer	wayside	daylight	away	bay	way
crayon	payment		play	stay	pray
maybe	rayon		may	birthday	lay
			today	highway	gay

A Vowel Sound: Schwa (announce)

(initial)

(initial)					
about	ago	America	appear	again	another
above	alone	alike	away	ahead	agree

"The Reading Teacher's Book of Lists, © 1984 Prentice-Hall, Inc., Englewood Cliffs, NJ 07632. By E. Fry, J. Polk, and D. Fountoukidis."

A Vowel Sound: Schwa (Announce) cont.

(medial)				(final)	
several	thousand	canvas	purchase	antenna	china
national	magazine	familiar	compass	algebra	comma
senator	breakfast	career	diagram	alfalfa	idea
				banana	

AL Vowel Sound: Broad O (ball)

(initial)		(medial)		(final)	
all	altogether	talk	scald	call	baseball
always	alternate	walk	walnut	tall	wall
also	altar	chalk	fallen	fall	stall
already	albeit	salt		overall	recall
almost	almanac	false		hall	
although	almighty	falter		small	

AU Vowel Sound: Broad O (auto)

(initial)			(medial)		
August	Australia	audible	because	cause	launch
author	autoharp	authentic	caught	dinosaur	faucet
autumn	auction	auditor	laundry	sauce	sausage
auditorium	auburn		haul	caution	overhaul
autograph	auxilliary		daughter	exhaust	
audience	automatic		fault	fraud	

AW Vowel Sound: Broad O (saw)

(initial)	(medial)			(final)	
awful	lawn	yawn	crawl	law	paw
awkward	drawn	tawny	squawk	jaw	claw
awning	lawyer	drawer	scrawl	draw	flaw
awe	hawk	shawl		straw	gnaw
awl	lawful	bawl		thaw	caw
awfully				taw	

AR Vowel Sound: AIR Sound (library)

(initial)	(medial)				
area	January	secretary	tiara	scare	beware
	dictionary	canary	parent	scarcely	flare
	vary	daring	wary	declare	
	primary	February	careful		

"The Reading Teacher's Book of Lists," © 1984 Prentice-Hall, Inc., Englewood Cliffs, NJ 07632. By E. Fry, J. Polk, and D. Fountoukidis."

AR Vowel Sound: Air sound (Library) cont.

(final)

care	share	bare	fare	glare	hare
rare	spare	dare	stare	welfare	square
aware					

AR Vowel Sound: AR Sound (star)

(initial)		**(medial)**		**(final)**	
are	argument	card	garden	car	mar
arm	article	March	start	far	par
army	arch	farm	dark	bar	scar
art	armor	hard	yard	jar	
artist	ark	part	party	tar	
arctic	arbor	large			

B Consonant Sound: Regular (book)

(initial)		**(medial)**		**(final)**	
be	back	number	subject	tub	job
by	but	problem	baby	cab	club
boy	because	remember		rob	rub
been	below	object		cub	grab
box	before	probably		rib	adverb
big	better			verb	bulb

BL Consonant Sound: BL Blend (block)

(initial)				**(medial)**	
black	blame	blank	blink	oblige	obliterate
blue	bloom	blast	blur	emblem	grumbling
bleed	blossom	blend	blow	tumbler	oblivious
blood	blond	blew	blanket	nosebleed	gamber
blind	blade	blot	bleach	ablaze	rambling
				nimbly	

BR Consonant Sound: Blend (broom)

(initial)			**(medial)**		
bread	bring	brush	library	daybreak	algebra
break	breath	breeze	umbrella	cobra	embrace
brick	branch	bridge	celebrate	membrane	lubricate
broad	bright	brain	vibrate	outbreak	
brother	broken	brass	abroad	zebra	
brown	brave	breakfast			

C Consonant Sound: Regular (K Sound) (Cat)

(initial)		(medial)		(final)	
can	call	because	across	back	check
come	country	picture	become	rock	stick
came	cut	American	quickly	sick	black
camp	car	second		lock	pick
color	cold			kick	thick
could	carry			music	electric

C Consonant Sound: S Sound (City)

(initial)			(medial)		
cent	certain	cigar	face	decide	acid
circle	civil	cyclone	since	Pacific	dancing
cycle	ceiling	cellar	pencil	percent	peaceful
circus	celebrate	cease	fancy	precise	
center	cereal		ice	process	
cell	cinder		concert	sincere	

CH Consonant Sound: Digraph (Chair)

(initial)		(medial)		(final)	
children	chief	pitcher	searching	which	catch
church	chart	attached	stretched	each	branch
change	chin	purchase	exchange	much	touch
chance	chest	merchant		such	inch
cheer	chain			teach	reach
check	chase			rich	watch

CL Consonant Sound: CL Blend (Clock)

(initial)				(medial)		
clean	clear	clever	climb	enclose	eclipse	disclose
cloth	class	cliff	click	include	acclaim	decline
clay	clap	close		cyclone	conclude	proclaim
claim	claws	cloud		exclaim	reclaim	incline
club	clerk	clues		exclude	declare	

CR Consonant Sound: CR Blend (Crab)

(initial)					
cry	crash	crazy	create	crayon	cruel
crack	cream	cross	cried	creek	credit
crowd	crew	crow	crops	crown	

CR Consonant Sound CR Blend (Crab) cont.

(medial)

across	microscope	aircraft	concrete	decree	scarecrow
secret	democrat	sacred	decrease	recruit	screen
increase					

D Consonant Sound: Regular (Dog)

(initial)		(medial)		(final)	
do	does	study	order	and	find
day	door	under	Indians	good	need
did	done	idea	didn't	had	did
dear	different	body		said	old
down	during			red	around
deep	don't			would	end

DR Consonant Sound: DR Blend (Drum)

(initial)			(medial)		
dry	dream	drift	address	undress	hydrogen
draw	dragon	drama	hundred	withdraw	laundress
drug	drill	drain	children	daydream	redress
drove	drink	drip	dandruff	eardrum	dewdrop
drop	drive	drench	cathedral	laundry	
dress	drew	droop			

E Vowel Sound: Short (Elephant)

(initial)			(medial)			
end	empty	ever	when	let	set	men
egg	energy	edge	then	them	went	spell
every	explain	enter	get	very	help	next
extra	enjoy	elf	left	tell	well	red
enemy	engine	else				

E Vowel Sound: Long Open Syllable Rule (Egypt)

(initial)	(medial)			(final)	
even	cedar	meter	being	me	we
equal	demon	prefix	recent	he	be
ether	secret	react	legal	she	maybe
evil	Negro	area	really		
ecology	zebra	female	depot		

"The Reading Teacher's Book of Lists, © 1984 Prentice-Hall, Inc., Englewood Cliffs, NJ 07632. By E. Fry, J. Polk, and D. Fountoukidis."

EE Vowel Sound: Long E (Deer)

(initial)   **(medial)**   **(final)**

(initial)	(medial)		(final)		
eel	sleep	seem	see	bee	fee
eerie	green	teeth	three	degree	spree
	keep	sweet	tree	flee	referee
	street	week	free	knee	
	feet	screen	agree	glee	
	wheel	fifteen			
	feel				

EA Vowel Sound: Long E (Peach)

(initial)			(medial)		(final)
eat	eager	ease	neat	leaf	sea
each	easel	eaves	read	feast	tea
east	Easter	easily	least	peach	flea
easy	eaten		beat	meat	plea
eagle	eastern		clean	weak	pea
			deal	peanut	

EA Vowel Sound: Short E Sound (Bread)

(medial)

head	breath	feather	meadow	threaten	heaven
heavy	deaf	death	pleasant	treasure	dread
ready	ahead	measure	spread	weapon	pleasure
thread	breakfast	instead	heading	weather	widespread
steady	already	leather	sweat	overhead	gingerbread
dead					

E Vowel Sound: Schwa (Eleven)

(initial)		(medial)			
efface	effective	happen	scientist	fuel	label
effect	efficient	problem	item	given	absent
efficiency		hundred	united	level	agent
erratic		arithmetic	quiet	heaven	hundred
essential		children	diet	even	often
erroneous		calendar	different	happen	

E Vowel Sound: Silent (Whale)

(medial)

sometimes	statement	movement	homework	something
careful	safety	moreover	lifetime	evening

"The Reading Teacher's Book of Lists," © 1984 Prentice-Hall, Inc., Englewood Cliffs, NJ 07632. By E. Fry, J. Polk, and D. Fountoukidis."

E Vowel Sound: Silent (Whale) cont.

(final)

are	little	here	make	people	home
one	like	came	time	place	
there	were	these	more	sentence	
come	before	some	write	because	

ER Vowel Sound: R Sound (Letter)

(medial)		(final)			
camera	afternoon	her	better	another	river
allergy	liberty	mother	sister	baker	winter
bakery	operate	over	under	wonder	liver
wonderful	federal	other	after	ever	shower
dangerous	battery	were	water	offer	lower

F Consonant Sound: Regular (Fish)

(initial)		(medial)		(final)	
for	father	after	different	if	chief
first	face	before	Africa	half	stuff
find	family	often	beautiful	myself	brief
four	follow	careful		off	cliff
funny	far			leaf	itself
food	few			himself	wolf

FL Consonant Sound: FL Blend (Flag)

(initial)				(medial)	
flower	floor	fleet	flea	afflict	inflame
flat	flavor	flow	fluffy	inflict	afloat
flight	flood	flap		conflict	reflect
flew	flute	flock		influence	inflate
fly	flame	fling		aflame	inflexible
float	flash	flip		snowflake	

FR Consonant Sound: FR Blend (Frog)

(initial)				(medial)	
free	frost	fruit	frisky	afraid	defraud
from	frank	freedom		affront	infringe
front	freshman	frozen		befriend	leapfrog
friend	frame	France		bullfrog	refrain
Friday	fresh	freighter		carefree	refresh
fry	fraction	fragile		confront	infrequent

G Consonant Sound: Regular (Gate)

(initial)		(medial)		(final)	
go	gun	again	segment	dog	frog
good	game	ago	regular	big	pig
got	gas	began	figure	egg	log
gave	gift	sugar		leg	bag
girl	gone	wagon		fig	
get	garden	signal		flag	

G Consonant Sound: J Sound (Giant)

(initial)			(medial)	(final)	
gem	gym	gesture	danger	change	page
giraffe	gypsy	genius	energy	large	village
gentlemen	ginger	genuine	region	bridge	huge
geography	gelatin	generate	engine	age	strange
generous	germ		original		
gently	general		vegetable		
			oxygen		

GL Consonant Sound: GL Blend (Glass)

(initial)				(medial)	
glad	glisten	glare	glider	eyeglass	hourglass
globe	gloom	glass	glimpse	jingling	bugler
glow	glue	glade	glitter	spyglass	angler
glory	glum	gleam	glance	smuggling	mangling
glove	glamour	glee	glaze	wiggling	singly

GR Consonant Sound: Blend (Grapes)

(initial)					
grade	grand	grant	(medial)		
great	green	grin	hungry	Negro	disgrace
grow	ground	gradual	angry	program	fragrant
grew	group	grandfather	congress	regret	outgrow
grass	grab	gravity	agree	degrade	engross
gray	grain		degree	engrave	

GH: Silent (Eight)

(medial)					
daughter	brighter	highway	night	fight	thought
might	throughout	eighth	neighbors	thoroughly	delight

"The Reading Teacher's Book of Lists," © 1984 Prentice-Hall, Inc., Englewood Cliffs, NJ 07632. By E. Fry, J. Polk, and D. Fountoukidis."

GH: Silent (Eight) cont.

(medial) cont.   (final)

light	fought	high	through	sleigh	dough
right	bought	sigh	weigh	although	neigh
sight	caught	bough	though	plough	
tight	taught				

H Consonant Sound: Regular (Hand)

(initial)   (medial)

he	help	half	high	behind	rehearse
had	here	his	hit	ahead	behold
have	happy	hen	house	unhappy	unhook
her	home	hero		behave	ahoy
him	hard	hide		overhead	
how	has	hill		autoharp	

I Vowel Sound: Short (Indian)

(initial)   (medial)

in	it	ill	with	will	different
is	invent	include	did	big	until
if	important	India	this	still	miss
into	insect	isn't	little	give	begin
inch	instead	inside	which	his	city
			him		

I Vowel Sound: Long Open Syllable Rule (Iron)

(initial)   (medial)

I	icy	bicycle	pilot	variety	title
idea	Irish	tiny	quiet	dinosaur	spider
I'll	iodine	silent	triangle	giant	diagram
iris	Iowa	rifle	climate	lion	China
I'm	ivory				
item					

I—E Vowel Sound: Long Final E Rule (Ice)

(initial)   (medial)

idle	five	fire	nine	mile	drive
ire	white	write	bite	size	wire
isle	ride	life	like	wide	mine
I've	time	side	line	describe	wife

IR Vowel Sound: R Sound (Girl)

(medial)   **(final)**

girl	skirt	thirteen	shirk	circuit	fir
first	birthday	girth	mirth	girdle	sir
third	thirsty	birth	confirm	stirrup	stir
shirt	affirm	circus	Virginia	dirty	tapir
dirt	circle	thirty	firm		whir
					astir

J Consonant Sound: Regular (Jar)

(initial)   **(medial)**

just	jet	June	object	project	unjust
jump	job	jungle	enjoy	adjust	majesty
January	joke	junior	subject	dejected	majority
jaw	joy	jacket	major	overjoyed	rejoice
July	juice	join	banjo	adjoin	
			adjective	reject	

K Consonant Sound: Regular (Kite)

(initial)   **(medial)**   **(final)**

kind	kiss	monkey	market	like	work
key	kitten	broken	packing	make	mark
kill	kid	turkey	stroking	book	speak
king	kettle	worker		look	milk
keep	kick			cake	bank
kin	keen			cook	break

KN Consonant Sound: N (Knife)

(initial)   **(medial)**

knee	knelt	knack	knockout	knell	unknown
knew	knit	kneel	knickers	kneecap	doorknob
know	knock	knapsack	knothole	knives	penknife
knowledge	knight	knob	knoll	knotty	acknowledge
knot	knuckle	knead	knave	known	knick knack
					knock-kneed

L Consonant Sound: Regular (Letter)

(initial)

little	long	live	large	line	left
like	look	land	last	learn	light

L Consonant Sound: Regular (Letter) cont.

(medial)		(final)			
only	really	will	school	oil	spell
below	follow	all	shall	tell	well
along	family	girl	small	until	vowel
children					

M Consonant Sound: Regular (Man)

(initial)		(medial)		(final)	
me	more	number	important	from	farm
my	mother	American	example	them	room
make	move	something	family	am	arm
much	must	complete		seem	team
many	made			warm	form
may	men			him	bottom

N Consonant Sound: Regular (Nut)

(initial)		(medial)		(final)	
not	name	many	until	in	man
no	number	under	any	on	even
new	need	answer	animal	can	own
night	never	country		when	open
next	near			an	been
now	next			then	than

NG Consonant Sound: NG (King)

(medial)		(final)			
slingshot	gangster	sing	long	bang	spring
lengthen	singer	bring	song	lung	strong
longing	hanger	thing	gang	wing	fang
kingdom	gangplank	going	hang	ring	hung
youngster	gangway	swing	young	fling	string
					wrong

O Vowel Sound: Short (Box)

(initial)					
odd	opposite	October	opera	operate	opportunity
olive	oxen	occupy	oxygen	on	

O Vowel Sound: Short (Box) cont.

(medial)

not	body	pot	got	product	copy
box	fox	clock	problem	rock	job
hot	drop	follow	top	bottom	cannot
stop	pop				

O Vowel Sound: Long Open Syllable Rule (Radio)

(initial)		(medial)	(final)		
open	odor	October	go	zero	echo
over	omit	program	no	cargo	volcano
obey	oboe	Roman	so	piano	
ocean	okra	moment	hello	Negro	
Ohio		poem	ago	potato	
		total	also	hero	
		broken	auto		

O—E Vowel Sound: Long Final E Rule (Rope)

(initial)	(medial)				
owe	home	rode	whole	rose	stove
	those	nose	slope	spoke	awoke
	hope	stone	bone	smoke	phone
	note	joke	tone	drove	
	along	globe	pole	vote	

OA Vowel Sound: Long O (Boat)

(initial)	(medial)				
oak	coat	toast	approach	croak	coal
oat	soap	goat	loaf	soak	toad
oath	road	goal	groan	cloak	moan
oatmeal	coast	loan	foam	roach	throat
oaf	load	float	roast	boast	coach

OW Vowel Sound: Long O (Window)

(initial)		(medial)			(final)
own	owner	bowl	towboat	mower	show
owe		stowaway	crowbar		low
owing		snowball	bowling		slow

OW Vowel Sound: Long O (Window) cont.

(final) cont.

snow	follow	blow	mow	know	arrow
row	tomorrow	grow	glow	crow	borrow
yellow	throw	flow			

OW Vowel Sound: OU Diphthong (Owl)

(medial)   (final)

down	crown	towel	how	somehow	endow
town	cowboy	powder	now	eyebrow	vow
brown	power	tower	cow	bow	prow
flower	vowel	chowder	plow	scow	avow
crowd	downward	shower	allow	sow	snowplow

OY Vowel Sound: OI Diphthong (Boy)

(initial)   (medial)   (final)

oyster	royal	joyous	toy	decoy	convoy
	voyage	disloyal	joy	newsboy	envoy
	loyal	loyalty	enjoy	annoy	corduroy
	boycott	enjoyment	employ	soy	
	annoying	joyful	destroy	viceroy	
	employer	boyish	coy	Troy	
	boyhood		cowboy	alloy	

O Vowel Sound: Schwa (Violin)

(initial)   (medial)   (final)

other	oblige	mother	action	kimono
original	obstruct	money	canyon	
official	oppose	atom	weapon	
observe	occasion	second	period	
opinion	oppress	nation	mission	
objection	opossum	method	riot	

OI Vowel Sound: OI Diphthong (Oil)

(initial)   (medial)

oilcloth	ointment	join	coin	broil	poison
oilwell		point	choice	spoil	boil
oily		voice	noise	avoid	turmoil

"The Reading Teacher's Book of Lists, © 1984 Prentice-Hall, Inc., Englewood Cliffs, NJ 07632. By E. Fry, J. Polk, and D. Fountoukidis."

OI Vowel Sound: OI Diphthong (Oil) cont.

(medial) cont.

coil	exploit	sirloin	void	rejoice	embroider
moisture	doily	disappoint	broiler	joint	typhoid
appoint	soil	toil			

OU Vowel Sound: OU Diphthong (House)

(initial)		(medial)			(final)
out	outer	hour	aloud	doubt	thou
our	outline	sound	found	count	
ounce	outside	about	council	boundary	
oust	outlook	around	ground		
ourselves	outcry	round	loud		
outdoors	outfield	scout	cloud		
ouch		amount	mountain		

O Vowel Sound: Broad O (Dog)

(initial)			(medial)		
off	onto	offhand	soft	wrong	moth
office	offset	offshore	log	cloth	frost
officer	offspring	ostrich	long	toss	cross
often	onward		along	coffee	belong
on	onset		cost	strong	
offer	oncoming		across	song	

OR Vowel Sound: OR Sound (Fork)

(initial)		(medial)			(final)
or	Oregon	short	score	corner	for
order	organ	horn	form	store	more
ore	ordinary	fork	before	north	nor
orbit	oral	forget	horse	force	
orchestra	orchard	born	story		
ordinary	orchid	cord	important		

OO Vowel Sound: 1-Dot U, or Short OO (Book)

(medial)

look	took	foot	shook	brook	cook
good	wood	stood	goodbye	wool	dogwood

OO Vowel Sound: 1-Dot U, or Short OO (Book) cont.
(medial) cont.

hook	rook	soot	lookout	notebook	rookie
afoot	hoof	cookie	football	understood	handbook
hood	crook	nook	wooden	neighborhood	overlook
motherhood					

OO Vowel Sound: 2-Dot U, or Long OO (Moon)

(initial)	(medial)			(final)	
ooze	soon	tooth	mood	too	bamboo
	school	cool	roof	zoo	cuckoo
	room	goose	loose	shampoo	boo
	food	troop	balloon	woo	igloo
	shoot	fool	noon	coo	
	smooth	boot		tattoo	
	pool	tool		kangaroo	

P Consonant Sound: Regular (Pencil)

(initial)		(medial)		(final)	
put	point	open	perhaps	up	ship
people	piece	example	happy	sleep	top
page	pass	paper		jump	step
pair	person	important		help	map
part	paper	upon		stop	deep
picture	pull			group	drop

PH Consonant Sound: F (Telephone)

(initial)		(medial)		(final)	
photo	phase	alphabet	cellophane	photograph	telegraph
phonics	phantom	orphan	emphasis	phonograph	graph
phrase	phonetic	nephew	gopher	autograph	triumph
physical	pharmacy	sulphur	graphic	paragraph	
physician	phoenix	trophy	trophy		
pheasant	phenomenon	geography	sophomore		

PL Consonant Sound: PL Blend (Plate)

(initial)

play	please	place	planets	player	plank
plant	plow	plan	plastic	pleasant	plug
plain	plus	plane	platform	plot	

PL Consonant Sound: PL Blend (Plate) cont.

(medial)

supply	reply	display	supplying	airplane	apply
multiply	perplex	explain	surplus	applaud	complain
employ	imply				

PR Consonant Sound: Blend (Propeller)

(initial)   (medial)

pretty	president	present	probably	surprise	approach
price	prince	problem	prove	April	approximate
press	program	produce	pray	improve	appropriate
prize	practice	property	products	apron	impression
print	prepare	provide		express	

Q Consonant Sound: KW Sound (Queen)

(initial)   (medial)

quart	quiet	quote	square	liquid	squirm
quite	quack	quill	equal	equipment	sequence
question	quail	quality	squirrel	equator	squeak
quick	quake		frequent	equivalent	inquire
quit	quilt		require	squash	
queer	quiz		equation	earthquake	

R Consonant Sound: Regular (Ring)

(initial)   (medial)   (final)

run	rest	very	large	our	other
red	ride	part	story	their	over
right	road	word	form	for	water
ran	rock	around		year	her
read	room			dear	after
rat	rod			your	near

S Consonant Sound: Regular (Saw)

(initial)   (medial)   (final)

some	set	same	also	question	this
so	sound	sea	person	inside	us
see	say		answer	system	likes
said	sentence		himself		makes
soon	side				yes

S Consonant Sound: Regular (Saw) cont.

(final) cont.

miss	across	gas	perhaps
less	its	bus	

S Consonant Sound: Z Sound (Eyes)

(medial)   (final)

music	observe	please	is	ods	news
easy	museum	cheese	as	says	hers
busy	present	wise	was	suds	does
those	result	these	his	yours	
because	season		has	tongs	
desert	poison		ours	days	

SC Consonant Sound: SC Blend (Scale)

(initial)   (medial)

score	scatter	scream	scoop	describe	inscribe
school	scholar	scallop	scrub	telescope	unscramble
screen	scout	screw		description	microscopic
scratch	scarce	scared		microscope	unscrupulous
scarf	scramble	scab		nondescript	telescoping
scar	scrape			unscrew	descriptive

SH Consonant Sound: Digraph (Shoe)

(initial)   (medial)   (final)

she	shot	dashed	ashes	wish	rush
shall	shirt	splashing	friendship	wash	dish
show	shell	sunshine		fish	crash
ship	sheet	worship		push	bush
short	shop	fisherman		finish	flash
shape	shut			fresh	establish

SK Consonant Sound: SK Blend (Skate)

(initial)

sky	skunk	skeleton	sketch	skillet	skylark
skin	skirt	skull	ski	skirmish	skeptic
skill	skip	skid	skim	skinny	

SK Consonant Sound: SK blend (Skate) cont.

(medial)			(final)		
outskirts	numskull	muskmelon	desk	brisk	husk
askew	rollerskate	masked	task	mask	dusk
muskrat			ask		

SL Consonant Sound: SL Blend (Slide)

(initial)				(medial)	
slow	sled	slope	sly	asleep	oversleep
sleep	slave	slam	slash	landslide	snowslide
slept	sleeve	slate	slab	onslaught	grandslam
slip	slant	slipper	sleek	enslave	nonslip
slid	slice	sleet	slimy	bobsled	
slap	slight	slim		manslaughter	

SM Consonant Sound: SM Blend (Smoke)

(initial)					(medial)
smile	smash	smock	smote	smuggler	blacksmith
smooth	smear	smoky	smokestack	smattering	gunsmith
smell	smith	smudge	smelt	smorgasbord	silversmith
small	smolder	smuggle	smite		locksmith
smart	smack	smug	smithy		
smother	smog	smitten	smoker		

SN Consonant Sound: SN Blend (Snake)

(Initial)					
snow	snuggle	snapshot	sniff	snooze	snuff
snowball	snip	sneak	sniffle	snorkel	snowman
snare	snarl	snatch	snipe	snort	sniper
sneeze	snap	sneakers	snob	snout	snowy
snore	snack	sneer	snoop	snub	
snug	snail				

SP Consonant Sound: SP Blend (Spoon)

(initial)			
sports	spread	spot	spider
space	special	spin	spend
speak	speed	spoke	spark
spring	spell	spare	

SP Consonant Sound: SP Blend (Spoon) cont.

(medial)			(final)		
inspect	despise	despair	clasp	grasp	lisp
respect	inspire	unspeakable	crisp	wasp	wisp
respond	respectful	despite	gasp		

ST Consonant Sound: ST Blend (Stamp)

(initial)			(medial)		(final)
stop	story	stick	instead	restless	best
step	street	stone	destroy	poster	cast
stay	stand	stood	restore	destruction	dust
state	star		westward		fast
still	study		haystack		least
store	strong		tasty		past
					west

SW Consonant Sound: SW Blend (Swing)

(initial)					
swim	switch	sweet	swollen	swampy	swarthy
swell	swallow	swift	sway	swirl	swat
swept	swung	swan	swine	swarm	swerve
sweat	swam	swagger	swoop	swear	sworn
sweater	swamp	swap	swindle	swelter	swish
sweep					

T Consonant Sound: Regular (Top)

(initial)		(medial)		(final)	
to	took	city	later	not	what
two	table	into	sentence	at	set
take	ten	water	until	it	part
tell	talk	after		out	got
too	today			get	put
time	told			but	want

TH Consonant Sound: Digraph Voiceless (Three)

(initial)			(medial)		
thank	thirty	threw	something	athlete	toothbrush
think	thick	thumb	author	faithful	python
thing	thought	thunder	nothing	bathtub	
third	thread	threat			

TH Consonant Sound: Diagraph Voiceless (Three) cont.

(final)

with	worth	teeth	death	fifth
both	cloth	truth	south	bath
ninth				

TH Consonant Sound: Digraph Voiced (Feather)

(initial)		**(medial)**		**(final)**
the	though	mother	weather	smooth
that	thus	other	gather	
them	thy	brother	breathing	
they	thence	father	rhythm	
this	their	although	farther	
there	then	bother	leather	
than	thou	clothing	northern	
these		either		

TR Consonant Sound: Blend (Truck)

(initial)			**(medial)**		
track	trick	trouble	extra	control	country
tractor	travel	trap	electric	sentry	patrol
train	tree	trail	central	waitress	
trade	trim	triangle	attract	contract	
truly	trip	traffic	entry	patron	
try	true		subtract	contrast	

TW Consonant Sound: TW Blend (Twins)

(initial)					**(medial)**
twelve	twirl	twinkle	twinge	twelfth	between
twenty	twine	twist	twang	twill	entwine
twice	tweed	twitter	twentieth	twiddle	untwist
twig	twilight	twitch	tweet		intertwine

U Vowel Sound: Short (Umbrella)

(initial)			**(medial)**		
up	unhappy	unless	but	number	such
us	upon	umpire	run	must	hunt
under	usher		much	study	summer
until	unusual		just	hundred	jump
ugly	uproar		cut	sudden	gun
uncle	upset		funny	sun	

U Vowel Sound: Long Open Syllable Rule (Music)

(initial)		(medial)		(final)
unit	unify	future	humid	fugitive	menu
united	unique	human	museum	funeral
university	utilize	valuable	continuous	beautiful
uniform		humor	communicate	unusual
universe		January	bugle	musician
usual		pupil	cubic	puny
Utah		community	fuel	

U Vowel Sound: 1-Dot U (Bull)

(medial)

bullet	bush	cushion	bulls-eye	pulpit	bulldog
full	bushel	ambush	bushy	fully	armful
pull	sugar	bulletin	pullet	bullfrog	bully
push	pudding	handful	pushcart	fulfill	bullfight
put	butcher	pulley	bulldozer	bulwark	output

U Vowel Sound: 2-Dot U (Ruler)

(medial)

June	flute	tune	punctuation	revolution	tuna
July	prune	conclusion	constitution	ruby	influence
truth	parachute	tube	duty	prudent	solution
junior	cruel	February	nutrition	situation	rhubarb
rule	numeral	aluminum	reduce	ruin	truly
crude					

UR Vowel Sound: R Sound (church)

(initial)	(medial)			(final)	
urn	turn	purple	further	fur	spur
urban	burn	hurt	purpose	sulfur	cur
urchin	hurry	turkey	burst	murmur	bur
urge	curl	curb	surf	concur	
urgent	Thursday	nurse	turtle	occur	
	purse	surface		slur	

V Consonant Sound: Regular (valentine)

(initial)

very	voice	view	vowel	verb	violin
visit	vote	vest	van	vase	valley

"*The Reading Teacher's Book of Lists*, © 1984 Prentice-Hall, Inc., Englewood Cliffs, NJ 07632. By E. Fry, J. Polk, and D. Fountoukidis."

V Consonant Sound: Regular (Valentine) cont.

(medial)		(final)			
over	however	give	gave	live	leave
even	cover	five	twelve	move	wave
never	several	love	have	above	believe
river					

W Consonant Sound: Regular (window)

(initial)			(medial)		
we	water	would	away	awake	halfway
with	way	wave	reward	aware	sidewalk
will	were	win	forward	unwind	upward
was	word	woman	want	highway	midway
work	week	wait	sandwich	backward	tapeworm

WH Consonant Sound: Digraph (HW Blend) (wheel)

(initial)				(medial)	
when	white	whip	whiskey	awhile	buckwheat
what	while	whisper	whack	bobwhite	cartwheel
which	why	whistle	whiff	overwhelm	somewhere
whether	wheat	wheeze	whimper	somewhat	anywhere
where	whale	wharf	whiz	everywhere	nowhere
				meanwhile	

WR Consonant Sound: R (wrench)

(initial)				(medial)	
write	wrestle	wretch	wrung	awry	typewriter
writing	wrist	wrinkle	wry	rewrite	monkeywrench
written	wreath	wrapper	wrangle	handwriting	typewritten
wrote	wring	wrathful		unwrap	
wrong	wreck	wreckage		playwright	
wrap	wren	wriggle		shipwreck	

X Consonant Sound: KS Sound (box)

(medial)		(final)			
Mexico	explain	fox	fix	complex	vex
Texas	axis	ax	relax	index	wax
mixture	oxen	six	next	lax	sex
extremely	extra	tax	mix	hex	perplex
sixty	excuse	ox	prefix	lox	
expert	exclaim				

"The Reading Teacher's Book of Lists, © 1984 Prentice-Hall, Inc., Englewood Cliffs, NJ 07632. By E. Fry, J. Polk, and D. Fountoukidis."

Y Consonant Sound: Consonant (yarn)

(initial)   **(medial)**

you	youth	yam	yew	lawyer	vineyard
year	yawn	yank	yeast	canyon	papaya
yellow	yard	yak	yen	beyond	dooryard
yes	yet	yodel	yolk	courtyard	stockyard
yell	your	yacht	yonder	barnyard	backyard
young					

Y Vowel Sound: Long E (baby)

(medial)   **(final)**

anything	very	happy	country	early
babysit	any	lady	city	money
everyone	many	story	really	quickly
ladybug	pretty	family	body	heavy
bodyguard	only	study	usually	ready
copying	funny	every	easy	energy
everything				

Y Vowel Sound: Long I Sound (fly)

(medial)   **(final)**

myself	type	my	sky	shy	reply
nylon	lying	by	July	defy	sly
cycle	rhyme	why	fry	dry	deny
dying	python	buy	apply	ally	
style	hyena	cry	pry	spy	

Z Consonant Sound: Regular (zebra)

(initial)   **(medial)**   **(final)**

zero	zipper	lazy	citizen	size	quiz
zoo	zoom	crazy	frozen	freeze	whiz
zone		puzzle	breeze	prize	buzz
zest		dozen	grazing		fizz
zenith		magazine	organize		fuzz
zigzag		realize	seize		jazz
zinc					adz

"The Reading Teacher's Book of Lists," © 1984 Prentice-Hall, Inc., Englewood Cliffs, NJ 07632. By E. Fry, J. Polk, and D. Fountoukidis."

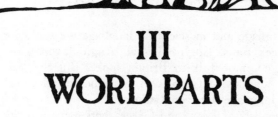

III
WORD PARTS

VOCABULARY BUILDING

In formal language and in scientific language we use a lot of words that have Latin or Greek roots. English has an Anglo-Saxon base (like German) which is what the common folk in Britain spoke. But the learned conquerors were the Romans, who spoke Latin with many borrowed Greek words. Thus, the more cultured language drew on Latin.

The following lists of Latin and Greek roots can form the basis for a vocabulary building course. They will help your students to understand many words that they already know, like *telephone,* and to extend them into words like *telepathy.*

These Latin- and Greek-based words are favorites for examination makers on all sorts of standardized tests.

But vocabulary building with these words should begin long before high school. Students come across terms like *hemisphere* and *automobile* in elementary school, and if some thoughtful teacher explains their roots, vocabulary building proceeds much faster throughout the school years. Roots often are taught successfully in families like *telephone, telegraph, television* to illustrate that *tele* means *far.*

Roots are suitable for discussions, either planned or spontaneous, and can be included in spelling lessons. Once they have been introduced, students should be given an opportunity to use them in sentences. Like any other lesson, they can be boring if overdone but fascinating if done with care and imagination.

Greek Roots

Root	Meaning	Examples
aero	air	aerial, aerodynamics
aesthet	perception	aesthetic
amphi	both ways	amphibious, amphitheater
anthro	man	anthropologist, philanthropist
ast	star	asterisk, astronomy, astrophysics
auto	self	automatic, automobile, autobiography
baro	weight	barometer
biblio	book	bibliography, Bible
bio	life	biology, biography
card	heart	cardiac
chrono	time	chronological, synchronize
cyclo	wheel	bicycle, cycle
demo	people	democracy

Root	Meaning	Examples
dont	teeth	orthodontist
gam	marriage	polygamy
geo	earth	geography, geometry, geology
graph, gram	write	telegraph, telegram, phonograph
gyn	woman	gynecologist
hemi	half	hemisphere
hetero	different	heterogeneous
homo	same	homogeneous, homogenized
hydro	water	hydroelectric
iatry	medical treatment	psychiatry, podiatry
kine, cine	move	kinetic, cinema
litho	stone	lithography, monolithic
log	word	prologue, apology, dialogue
mania	madness	maniac
mech	machine	mechanic, mechanical
mega	great	megaphone
meter	measure	barometer, thermometer
micro	small	microscope, microbe
mono	alone, one	monogamy, monarch, monologue
morph	shape	amorphous, metamorphosis
neo	new, recent	neoclassic, neophyte
opt	eye	optical, optometrist
ortho	straight	orthodontist, orthodox
paleo	old	paleolithic, paleontology
pan	all	panorama, panacea, pandemonium
para	beside, equal	parallel, compare, disparity
patho	suffering	pathology, sympathy
pod	foot	tripod, podiatry
ped	child	pediatrician
peri	around	perimeter, periscope
phil	love	philosophy, philanthropist
phob	fear	phobia, claustrophobia
phon	sound	phonetics, symphony, phonograph
photo	light	photography, photosynthesis
phys	nature	physical, physics
polis, polit	city	metropolis, cosmopolitan

Root	Meaning	Examples
poly	many	polygon, polygamy
pseud	false	pseudonym
psych	mind, soul	psychology, psyche
scope	see	microscope, telescope
tele	far	telephone, telegraph
theo	god	theology, atheism

Latin Roots

Root	Meaning	Examples
act	do	action, reaction, transact
alt	high	altitude, altimeter
ambi	both ways	ambidextrous, ambiguous
amo, ami	love	amiable, amorous
ang	bend	angle, rectangle
anim	feeling	animosity, animation
ann, enn	year	annual, anniversary, biennial
apt, ept	suitable	aptitude, ineptitude
aqua	water	aquarium, aquatic
art	skill	artisan, artistic
aud, audit	hear	auditorium, audition
bene	good	benefit, benediction
brev	short	abbreviate, brevity
cap	head	cap, captain, capital
cede, ceed	go	proceed, exceed, antecedent
ceive, cept	seize	receive, recepticle
cent	100	century, centipede
cent	center	centrifuge, centripetal
cert	sure	certain, certify
cide, cise	cut; kill	suicide, scissor, incisor
circ	around	circle, circular
clam, claim	shout	proclaim, clamor
clar	clear	clarity, declare
cline	lean	incline, recline, decline
clud, clos, clus	shut	include, closet, seclusion
cogn	know	recognize, cognition
corp	body	corporal, corporation, corps

Root	Meaning	Examples
cred	believe	credit, incredible
curr	run	current, occurrence
dict	speak	predict, dictator
domin	master	dominate, predominate
don, donat	give	donation, donor
equ	equal	equality, equilibrium
fac, fec, fic, *fy*	make, do	affect, modification, manufacture, classify
fer	carry	ferry, transfer
fict	pretend	fiction, fictitious
fid	faithful	fidelity, confidence
firm	fixed	infirm, confirm
flect, flex	bend	deflect, reflection, reflex
form	shape	conform, formula
fract, frag	break	fracture, fraction, fragment
frater	brother	fraternity
fuga, fugi	flee	fugitive, refugee
grad, gress	by steps	gradually, progress
grat	pleasing; thankful	grateful, congratulate
greg	gather	gregarious, congregation
hab	hold	habit, habitual
homo	man	homicide, homo sapiens
hosp	host	hospitality, hospice
imag	likeness	image, imagine
init	beginning	initial, initiate
ject	throw	reject, inject, project
junct	join	junction, conjunction
jus, jud, jur	law; right	justice, judicious, injury
lab	work	labor, laboratory
lat	carry	translate, relative
laud, plaud, *plaus*	strike	applause, plaudits
leg, lect	read	legible, intelligent, lecture
lev	raise	levitate, elevate, levity
lib	book; free	library, liberty
loc	place	location, dislocate

Root	Meaning	Examples
luc, lum, lus	bright	lucid, luminate, luster
luna	moon	lunar, lunatic
mag	great	magnify, magnitude
man	hand	manual manufacture, manuscript
mar	sea	marine, maritime, submarine
mater	mother	maternity, maternal
max	greatest	maximum
med, mid	middle	medium, middle, mediocre
mem	mindful	memory, remember
ment	mind	mental, mentor
merg, mers	dip; dive	submerge, submerse
mim	same	mimic, mimeograph
minist	servant	minister, administer
miss, mit	send	mission, missile, transmit
mort	death	mortician, immortal
mov, mot, mat	move	motor, automatic
multi	many	multitude, multiply
mut	change	mutation, immutable
narr	tell	narrate
nat	born	native, nation
nav	ship	navy, navigate
neg	deny	negation
not	mark	notation, denote
noun, nunc	announce	pronounce, denunciate
nov	new	novelty, novel
numer	number	numeral, enumerate
ocu	eye	oculist, binocular
opt	best	optimist, optimum
ord	row	orderly, extraordinary, ordinal
orig	begin	original, originate
pater	father	paternal, paternity
ped	foot	pedal, pedestrian
pell, puls	push	repellent, compulsory, propeller
pend, pens	hang	pendulum, suspense
plic, plex	interweave; fold	complicated, perplex, plexiglass
plur	more	plural

Root	Meaning	Examples
pop	people	population, popular
port	carry	portable, transport
pos, pon	place; put	position, postpone
post	after	post mortem, postscript
prehend, prehens	seize	comprehend, comprehension
prim, princ	first	primitive, principle, primary
pugn	fight	pugnacious, pugilist
put	think	reputation, disreputable
quer, ques, quis	seek	query, question, inquisitive
rad, ray	spoke; ray; root	radius, radiology, radiate
rect	straight	erect, rectify, direction
reg	king	regal, reign
rid	laugh	ridicule, deride
rupt	break	rupture, abrupt, bankrupt
san	healthy	sanitary, sane
scend	climb	ascend, descendant
scribe, script	write	scripture, inscribe
sect	cut	dissect, intersection
sens	feelings	sensible, sentimental, sensitive
serv	serve	servant, service
sess, set	sit	session, settle
sign	mark	signature, signal
sim	like	similar, simultaneous
sist, stat	stand	insist, status
sol	alone	solitary, solo
solv, solu	loosen	dissolve, solution
sono, sona	sound	sonorous, sonata
spec, spic	see	spectator, suspicion
spir	breathe	spirit, respiration
stell	star	stellar, constellation
stimu	whip	stimulation
strict	tighten	restrict, constrict
struct	build	construction, instructor
sum, sup	superior	supreme, summit
tact, tang	touch	intact, contact, tangible
temp	time	temporary, extemporaneous, tempt

Root	Meaning	Examples
ten, tend, tens	hold, stretch	retentive, tenacious, intend, tenant, tension, pretend, extensive
term	end	terminal, determine, exterminate
terr	land	terrain, territory
tex	weave	textile, texture
tort	twist	torture, contortion
tract	pull; drag	tractor, attraction, subtract
trans	across	transport, transcontinental
trib	give	contribute, tributary
trud, trus	push	intrude, protrusion
turb	confusion	disturb, turbulence
vag	wander	vagabond, vagrant
var	different	varied, invariably
ven, vent	come	invent, convention
vers, vert	turn	reverse, convert
vict, vinc	conquer	victory, convince
vis, vid	see	vision, evidence
viv, vit	live	vivid, survive, vitamin
voc	voice	vocal, advocate
volv	roll	revolver, revolutionary

WHAT COMES BEFORE AND AFTER CAN CHANGE THE WHOLE MEANING

Prefixes—small but meaningful letter groups added before a base word or root—change the meaning of a word. The change in meaning can be complete, as in *un* + *happy* = *unhappy* or *non* + *profit* = *nonprofit*. Or the change in meaning can clarify or make the word more specific, as in *pre* + *game* = *pregame* or *extra* + *sensory* = *extrasensory*.

Knowing the meaning of these prefixes, together with the meaning of common base words and Greek and Latin roots, will give students the tools for unlocking the meanings of hundreds of words.

Though you will want to make a point of teaching these prefixes directly, it is a good idea to explain prefixes and their meanings when your students encounter them in new vocabulary words throughout the year. Pointing out the prefixes and discussing what they add to the word meaning will be a review and a demonstration of their practical value.

Suffixes—letter groups that are added to the end of a base word or root—perform two services. First, they add information to the meaning of the word. This is the use that is more commonly thought of. For example, *drop* + *let* = *droplet* or *mend* + *able* = *mendable*.

Second, some suffixes help with grammar and syntax. Though not thought of as commonly, this is a very important function. Grammar and syntax suffixes fall into three categories: those that indicate part of speech, those that indicate number, and those that indicate time and tense.

Part of speech suffixes enable you to express an idea in many different ways using the variation of the key word that best fits the sentence structure. For example: The boy was *quiet*. The boy played *quietly*. The boy's *quietness* was undisturbed. *Quiet* was used as an adjective, an adverb, and a noun—with the help of suffixes.

Suffixes that indicate number are added to nouns to make the noun plural. Suffixes of time or tense are added to verbs to indicate when an action has occurred.

Teach suffixes and their meanings in groups with selected roots or base words. By combining and recombining the parts and discussing the meanings and grammar changes, students will become accustomed to looking at endings for information.

Prefixes Expressing Time and Place

in, into

in-, il-, im-, ir- (L.)

infiltrate, illuminate, import, irrigate

en- (Fr.)   enlist
intro- (L.)   introduce

inside, within

intro- (L.)   introspection
intra- (L.)   intravenous
endo- (Gk.)   endogenous

to, toward

ad-, ac-, ag-, at- (L.)   adjust, accommodate, aggression,
                                             attract

ob- (L.)   observe

forth, forward

pro- (L.)   proclaim

beside, by

para- (Gk.)   parallel, paraphrase

between, among

inter- (L.)   intervene
dia- (Gk.)   dialogue

outside

extra-, extro- (L.)   extraterrestrial, extrovert
epi- (Gk.)   epidermis

with, at the same time

com-, con-, cor- (L.)   company, contemporary, correlate
syn-, sym- (Gk.)   synchronize, symphony

after

post- (L.)   postwar, posterior

before

pre- (L.)   precede
ante- (L.)   antebellum
pro- (Gk.)   prologue

down

de- (L.)   descend

under, beneath

sub- (L.)   subway

above, over

super- (L.)   superior, supersensitive

back, backward

re- (L.)   retreat
retro- (L.)   retroactive

around, about

circum- (L.)   circumference
peri- (Gk.)   perimeter

through, throughout

per- (L.)   perennial

across

trans- (L.)   transport, transatlantic
dia- (Gk.)   diameter

beyond

ultra- (L.)   ultrasonic, ultraconservative
extra- (L.)   extraordinary, extrapolate

apart

se- (L.)   secular, separate

from, away from

ab-, abs- (L.)   absolve, abstain

off, away

dis-, di- (L.)   dismiss, divert

out, out of

ex- (L.)	exit, expel
ex-, ec- (Gk.)	exorcist, eccentric

Prefixes Expressing Negation and Reversal

not

un- (Eng.)	unpleasant
in-, il-, im-, ir- (L.)	indecisive, illogical, impolite, irrelevant
dis- (L.)	disapprove
non- (L.)	nonviolent
a- (Gk.)	atypical

reversal

un- (Eng.)	unsettle
de- (L.)	deregulate
dis- (L.)	disarm
counter- (L.)	countermand

Prefixes Expressing Number

one, single, alone

mono-, mon- (Gk.)	monorail, monocular
uni- (L.)	uniform

two, twice

di- (Gk.)	dioxide
bi-, bin- (L.)	bicycle, binocular

three

tri- (Gk., L.)	triangle

four

tetr- (Gk.)	tetrahedron
quadr- (L.)	quadrangle

"The Reading Teacher's Book of Lists, © 1984 Prentice-Hall, Inc., Englewood Cliffs, NJ 07632. By E. Fry, J. Polk, and D. Fountoukidis."

five

pent- (Gk.)   pentathlon
quintus- (L.)   quintuplet

six

hexa-, hex- (Gk.)   hexagon
sex- (L.)   sextet

seven

hept- (Gk.)   heptagon
sept-, septem- (L.)   September

eight

oct- (Gk., L.)   octet, October

nine

nove- (L., Gk.)   November, novena

ten, tenth

deca-, deka-, dec- (Gk.)   December, decameter
deci- (L.)   decimal

hundred, hundredth

centi-, cent- (L.)   century, cent

thousand, thousandth

milli- (L.)   millimeter
kilo- (Gk.)   kilometer, kilogram

many, much

poly- (Gk.)   polygon, polyester
multi- (L.)   multitude

first

prot- (Gk.)   proton, protagonist

half

hemi- (Gk.)   hemisphere
semi- (L.)   semicircle

Miscellaneous Prefixes

bad, badly

mal- (L.)   malpractice, malignant
mis- (L.)   misfit, miserable

wrong

mis- (L.)   misspell, mistake

good, well

bene- (L.)   benefactor, benign

common, like

homo- (Gk.)   homogeneous

like, same

syn- (Gk.)   synonymous

Noun Suffixes

1. One who _____. A student is one who studes.

-ant	servant
-ar	beggar
-ent	superintendent
-er	teacher
-ess	waitress
-or	actor

2. One who is _____. An employee is one who is employed.

-ard	drunkard
-ee	payee

3. One who practices _____. A scientist practices science.

-ist	anarchist

4. Place for or with _____. an aquarium is a place with water (aqua).

-arium	solarium
-ary	library
-orium	auditorium
-ory	laboratory

5. Art or skill of _____. Salesmanship is the skill of salesmen.

-ship	showmanship

6. State or quality of being _____. Tolerance is the state of being tolerant.

-ance	repentance
-ation	starvation
-dom	freedom
-ence	violence
-hood	childhood
-ion	champion
-ism	heroism
-ity	necessity
-ment	amusement
-ness	happiness
-ship	friendship
-sion	tension
-th	length
-tion	attention
-ty	loyalty
-ure	failure

7. Doctrine of _____. Marxism is the doctrine of Marx.

-ism	capitalism

8. Study of _____. Psychology is the study of the psyche.

-ology	biology

9. Small _____. A booklet is a small book.

-cle	particle
-cule	molecule
-ette	dinette
-let	rivulet

10. More than one _____. Cats means more than one cat.

-a	data
-s	buildings
-es	boxes
-i	alumni

Adjective Suffixes

1. Relating to _____. Commercial describes something related to commerce.

-al	natural
-an	urban
-ial	artificial
-ic	historic
-ical	comical

2. Inclined to _____. Combative describes someone inclined to combat.

-acious	voracious
-ant	vigilant
-ative	demonstrative
-ent	competent
-ish	childish
-ive	instructive

3. Can be _____. Something readable can be read.

-able	lovable
-ible	visible

4. Full of _____. A careful person is full of care.

-ful	thoughtful
-ous	wondrous
-ulent	turbulent
-y	wordy

5. Without _____. A careless person acts without care.

-less	thoughtless

6. That which was _____. Mistaken is that which someone mistook.

-ed	baked
-en	stolen

Adverb Suffixes

1. In what manner. Steadily means done in a steady manner.

-ily	speedily
-ly	slowly

2. To what extent. Extremely means done to an extreme.

-ly	scarcely

"The Reading Teacher's Book of Lists, © 1984 Prentice-Hall, Inc., Englewood Cliffs, NJ 07632. By E. Fry, J. Polk, and D. Fountoukidis."

Verb Suffixes

1. To make _____. Weak<u>en</u> means to make weak.

-ate	activate
-en	strengthen
-fy	terrify
-ize	popularize

2. To change tense or time. March<u>ed</u> means the action was done in the past.

-ed	talked
-en	taken
-ing	singing

SYLLABLES ARE CONTROVERSIAL

The teaching of syllabication rules is somewhat controversial. Some say you should, and some say it is not worth the effort. Syllables sometimes are part of phonics lessons because syllabication affects vowel sounds (for example, an open vowel rule), and sometimes they are part of spelling or English lessons. McGuffey and the New England Primer both made extensive use of syllables in teaching beginning reading. Modern teachers and teaching methods do not.

Syllables may or may not come back into favor as a teaching unit. In the meantime, dictionaries use them, and a few, mostly remedial, teaching methods use them.

We are presenting some common syllables and rules for breaking words into syllables as a reference. (There is no close agreement on various lists of syllabication rules, and some of the rules have plenty of exceptions.) We are not urging you to teach them, but neither are we urging you to refrain from doing so.

Common Syllables

These are the 322 most common unweighed nonword graphemic syllables in the English language, ranked in order of frequency.*

1	ing	15	ex		be
	er		al		per
	a		de	30	to
	ly		com		pro
5	ed		o		ac
	i				ad
	es	20	di		ar
	re		en	35	ers
	tion		an		ment
10	in		ty		or
	e		ry		tions
	con	25	u		ble
	y		ti	40	der
	ter		ri		ma

---

*Sakiey, Fry, Goss & Loldman (1980). Syllable Frequency Count. *Visible Language XIV*, 2.

	na		ci		cy
	si		mo		fa
	un	85	on	125	im
45	at		ous		li
	dis		pi		lo
	ca		se		men
	cal		ten		min
	man	90	tor	130	mon
50	ap		ver		op
	po		ber		out
	sion		can		rec
	vi		dy		ro
	el	95	et	135	sen
55	est		it		side
	la		mu		tal
	lar		no		tic
	pa		ple		ties
	ture	100	cu	140	ward
60	for		fac		age
	is		fer		ba
	mer		gen		but
	pe		ic		cit
	ra	105	land	145	cle
65	so		light		co
	ta		ob		cov
	as		of		da
	col		pos		dif
	fi	110	tain	150	ence
70	ful		den		ern
	ger		ings		eve
	low		mag		hap
	ni		ments		ies
	par	115	set	155	ket
75	son		some		lec
	tle		sub		main
	day		sur		mar
	ny		ters		mis
	pen	120	tu	160	my
80	pre		af		nal
	tive		au		ness
	car				

	ning		ure		sun
	n't		way		the
165	nu	205	ate	245	ting
	oc		bet		tra
	pres		bles		tures
	sup		bod		val
	te		cap		var
170	ted	210	cial	250	vid
	tem		cir		wil
	tin		cor		win
	tri		coun		won
	tro		cus		work
175	up	215	dan	255	act
	va		dle		ag
	ven		ef		air
	vis		end		als
	am		ent		bat
180	bor	220	ered	260	bi
	by		fin		cate
	cat		form		cen
	cent		go		char
	ev		har		come
185	gan	225	ish	265	cul
	gle		lands		ders
	head		let		east
	high		long		fect
	il		mat		fish
190	lu	230	meas	270	fix
	me		mem		gi
	nor		mul		grand
	part		ner		great
	por		play		heav
195	read	235	ples	275	ho
	rep		ply		hunt
	su		port		ion
	tend		press		its
	ther		sat		jo
200	ton	240	sec	280	lat
	try		ser		lead
	um		south		lect

	lent		ral		stand
	less		rect		sug
285	lin		ried		tel
	mal	300	round		tom
	mi		row	315	tors
	mil		sa		tract
	moth		sand		tray
290	near		self		us
	nel	305	sent		vel
	net		ship	320	west
	new		sim		where
	one		sions		writ
295	point		sis		
	prac	310	sons		

Syllabication Rules*

Rule 1. VCV†	A consonant between two vowels tends to go with the second vowel unless the first vowel is accented and short. Example: bro-ken, wag-on
Rule 2. VCCV	Divide two consonants between vowels unless they are a blend or digraph. Example: pic-ture, ush-er
Rule 3. VCCCV	When there are three consonants between two vowels, divide between the blend or the digraph and the other consonant. Example: an-gler
Rule 4. Affixes	Prefixes always form separate syllables (un-hap-py), and suffixes from separate syllables only in the following cases: a. The suffix -y tends to pick up the preceding consonant. Example: fligh-ty

*Source: P. Costigan, *A Validation of the Fry Syllabification Generalization.* Unpublished master's thesis. Rutgers University, New Brunswick, NJ, 1977. Available from ERIC.
†V = vowel; C = consonant.

b.   The suffix -ed tends to form a separate syllable
      only when it follows a root that ends in d or t.
Example: plant-ed.
c.   The suffix -s never forms a syllable except
      when it follows an e.
Example: at-oms, cours-es

Rule 5. Compounds   Always divide compound words.
                         Example: black-bird

Rule 6. Final le   Final le picks up the preceding consonant to form a
                         syllable.
                         Example: ta-ble

Rule 7. Vowel
Clusters   Do not split common vowel clusters, such as:
                         a.   R-controlled vowels (ar, er, ir, or, and ur).
                         Example: ar-ti-cle
                         b.   Long vowel digraphs (ea, ee, ai, oa, and ow).
                         Example: fea-ture
                         c.   Broad o clusters (au, aw, and al).
                         Example: au-di-ence
                         d.   Diphthongs (oi, oy, ou, and ow).
                         Example: thou-sand
                         e.   Double o like oo.
                         Example: moon, moon-shine

Rule 8. Vowel
Problems   Every syllable must have one and only one vowel
                         sound.
                         a.   The letter e at the end of a word is silent.
                         Example: come
                         b.   The letter y at the end or in the middle of a
                               word operates as a vowel.
                         Example: ver-y, cy-cle
                         c.   Two vowels together with separate sounds
                               form separate syllables.
                         Example: po-li-o

"The Reading Teacher's Book of Lists," © 1984 Prentice-Hall, Inc., Englewood Cliffs, NJ 07632. By E. Fry, J. Polk, and D. Fountoukidis."

IV
REFERENCE

IT PAYS TO KNOW ABBREVIATIONS

Because abbreviations are so widely used, it is important to know what the common ones stand for. Not knowing their meanings is a definite disadvantage when reading all kinds of materials. In addition to aiding in reading comprehension, using abbreviations saves time, space, and energy when we write. Students will find them especially useful when they are taking notes in class.

To give students practice in using abbreviations, make up crossword puzzles that use the abbreviations as clues, or read classified ads and apply abbreviation knowledge in a practical way.

The abbreviations for state names are listed together since many teach them as a group. The official postal abbreviations are listed first; these use two capital letters. Some of them are easy to remember, such as NY and FL. Others will take a bit of concentration to get straight, such as MI, MO, MS, MA, MT, and ME. The traditional state abbreviations also are listed. While your students are at it, it's not a bad idea for them to learn to spell the full name of each state.

State Abbreviations

Full Name	New	Old
Alabama	AL	Ala.
Alaska	AK	Alaska
Arizona	AZ	Ariz.
Arkansas	AR	Ark.
California	CA	Calif.
Colorado	CO	Colo.
Connecticut	CT	Conn.
Delaware	DE	Del.
Florida	FL	Fla.
Georgia	GA	Ga.
Hawaii	HI	Hawaii
Idaho	ID	Idaho
Illinois	IL	Ill.
Indiana	IN	Ind.
Iowa	IA	Iowa
Kansas	KS	Kans.
Kentucky	KY	Ky.
Louisiana	LA	La.
Maine	ME	Me.

"The Reading Teacher's Book of Lists, © 1984 Prentice-Hall, Inc., Englewood Cliffs, NJ 07632. By E. Fry, J. Polk, and D. Fountoukidis."

Full Name cont.	New cont.	Old cont.
Maryland	MD	Md.
Massachusetts	MA	Mass.
Michigan	MI	Mich.
Minnesota	MN	Minn.
Mississippi	MS	Miss.
Missouri	MO	Mo.
Montana	MT	Mont.
Nebraska	NE	Nebr.
Nevada	NV	Nev.
New Hampshire	NH	N.H.
New Jersey	NJ	N.J.
New Mexico	NM	N. Mex.
New York	NY	N.Y.
North Carolina	NC	N.C.
North Dakota	ND	N. Dak.
Ohio	OH	Ohio
Oklahoma	OK	Okla.
Oregon	OR	Oreg.
Pennsylvania	PA	Pa.
Rhode Island	RI	R.I.
South Carolina	SC	S.C.
South Dakota	SD	S.D.
Tennessee	TN	Tenn.
Texas	TX	Tex.
Utah	UT	Utah
Vermont	VT	Vt.
Virginia	VA	Va.
Washington	WA	Wash.
West Virginia	WV	W.Va.
Wisconsin	WI	Wisc.
Wyoming	WY	Wyo.

Commonly Used Abbreviations

acct.	account	adv.	adverb
A.D.	anno Domini (in the year of our Lord)	AKA	also known as
		a.m.	ante meridiem (morning)
adj.	adjective		
ad lib	ad libitum (improvise)	amt	amount

anon.	anonymous	ea.	each
ans.	answer	ed.	edition
Apr.	April	e.g.	exempli gratia (for example)
arith.	arithmetic		
assn.	association	elec.	electric
assoc.	association	Esq.	Esquire
asst.	assistant	et al.	et alii (and others)
atty.	attorney	etc.	et cetera (and others)
Aug.	August	ex.	example
ave.	avenue	F	Fahrenheit
		Feb.	February
B.A.	Bachelor of Arts	fem.	feminine
bib.	bibliography	fig.	figure
biog.	biography	freq.	frequency
bldg.	building	Fri.	Friday
B.S.	Bachelor of Science	ft.	foot
c	centimeter, centigrade	g	gram
cap.	capital	gal.	gallon
Capt.	Captain	Gen.	General
cc	cubic centimeter	govt.	government
cert.	certificate	H.M.S.	His (Her) Majesty's Ship
chap.	chapter		
Chas.	Charles	Hon.	Honorable
COD	cash on delivery	hosp.	hospital
Col.	Colonel	hr	hour
conj.	conjunction	H.R.H.	His (Her) Royal Highness
corp.	corporation		
CPA	Certified Public Accountant	ht	height
cu	cubic	ibid.	ibidem (in the same place)
D.C.	District of Columbia	id.	idem (the same)
D.D.	Doctor of Divinity	i.e.	id est (that is)
D.D.S.	Doctor of Dental Surgery	illus.	illustration
		in.	inch
Dec.	December	inc.	incorporated
dept.	department	incl.	including
diam.	diameter	intro	introduction
div.	division	IRS	Internal Revenue Service
doz.	dozen		

Jan.	January	p.m.	post meridiem
Jour.	Journal		(afternoon)
Jr.	junior	pop.	population
kg	kilogram	pp.	pages
KKK	Ku Klux Klan	pres.	president
		prin.	principal
lat.	latitude	pron.	pronoun
lb.	pound	pt.	pint
lieut.	lieutenant		
long.	longitude	qt.	quart
lt.	lieutenant	recd.	received
		ref.	referee; reference
M.A.	Master of Arts	rev.	reverend
mag.	magazine	RIP	rest in peace
masc.	masculine	R.N.	Registered Nurse
math	mathematics	RR	railroad
M.D.	Doctor of Medicine		
mdse.	merchandise	Sat.	Saturday
med.	medium	sci.	science
mgr.	manager	sec.	second
min.	minute	Sept.	September
misc.	miscellaneous	sgt.	sergeant
ml	milliliter	sing.	singular
mo.	month	sq.	square
mph	miles per hour	Sr.	Senior; Sister
Mr.	mister	St.	Street; Saint
Mrs.	mistress	subj.	subject
		Sun.	Sunday
neg.	negative	supt.	superintendent
neut.	neuter		
no.	number	tel.	telephone
Nov.	November	Thurs.	Thursday
		Tues.	Tuesday
Oct.	October		
opp.	opposite	univ.	university
oz.	ounce	USA	United States of
			America
p.	page		
pd.	paid	Wm.	William
Ph.D.	Doctor of Philosophy	wt.	weight
pkg.	package	yd.	yard
pl.	plural	yr.	year

"The Reading Teacher's Book of Lists, © 1984 Prentice-Hall, Inc., Englewood Cliffs, NJ 07632. By E. Fry, J. Polk, and D. Fountoukidis."

vet.	veterinarian; veteran	vs.	versus
vocab.	vocabulary	Wed.	Wednesday
vol.	volume	wk.	week

HOW DO YOU WRITE DOWN A PHONEME?

English and most of the European and African languages use the Latin (Roman) alphabet. However, since this alphabet doesn't describe English too well—that is, it does not have a perfect phoneme–grapheme (sound–symbol) correspondence—dictionary writers and others are concerned with a more perfect graphic representation of sounds and have modified the alphabet.

The main way dictionaries tell you how to pronounce a sound is with their own phonetic symbols. These symbols are regular Latin symbols whenever possible, but they extend the Latin alphabet by adding diacritical marks and special letter combinations. Though all dictionaries use similar phonetic symbols, no two are exactly the same. The first chart shows how four different dictionaries might do it. A valuable section of the chart contains the common and uncommon spellings for the sound (phonemes do have spellings just as words do). The more common phoneme spellings also can be found in section II of this book—this list is useful because it gives some of the rarer phoneme spellings.

ITA and DMS are special alphabet modifications for the purpose of teaching beginning reading by making the spelling of words more phonically regular. Experiments show that they work, but not much better than the traditional methods.

The table of alphabets shows how some other languages are written. If you want to have some fun, get your students to write their names and addresses using different alphabets.

The manual alphabet shows one way in which deaf persons communicate. (They also have a signing language that uses hand positions for whole words or concepts, and most can read lips to some extent.)

The Morse Code is still used by some radio hams, and Boy Scouts can send flashlight messages to each other by using it.

Phonetic Symbols

Common and Uncommon Spellings for Phonemes

hat, plaid	a	a	ă	a
age, aid, gaol, gauge, say, break, vain, they	ā	ā	ā	ā
care, air, where, pear, their	ã, er, ar	eər	âr	â(r)
father, heart, sergeant	ä	ä	ä	ä

"The Reading Teacher's Book of Lists, © 1984 Prentice-Hall, Inc., Englewood Cliffs, NJ 07632. By E. Fry, J. Polk, and D. Fountoukidis."

bad, rabbit	b	b	b	b
child, watch, righteous, question, virtuous	ch	ch	ch	ch̆
did, add, filled	d	d	d	d
many, aesthetic, said, says, let, bread, heifer, leopard, friend, bury	ē	ē	ĕ	ē
Caesar, quay, equal, team, bee, receive, people, key, machine, believe, phoenix	ē	ē	ē	ē
stern, pearl, first, word, journey, turn, myrtle	ėr	ər	ûr	û(r)
fat, effort, laugh, phrase	f	f	f	f
go, egg, ghost, guest, catalogue	g	g	g	g
he, who	h	h	h	h
wheat	hw	hw	hw	hw
England, been, bit, sieve, women, busy, build, hymn	i	i	ĭ	i
aisle, aye, height, eye, ice, lie, buy, sky	ī	ī	ī	ī
bridge, gradual, soldier, tragic, exaggerate, jam	j	j	j	j
coat, account, chemistry, back, acquire, sacque, kind, liquor	k	k	k	k
land, tell	l	l	l	l
drachm, paradigm, calm, me, climb, common, solemn	m	m	m	m
gnaw, knife, no, manner, pneumonia	n	n	n	n
ink, long, tongue	ng	ng	ng	n̂g
watch, hot	o	ä	ŏ	o

"*The Reading Teacher's Book of Lists*, © 1984 Prentice-Hall, Inc., Englewood Cliffs, NJ 07632. By E. Fry, J. Polk, and D. Fountoukidis."

beau, yeoman, sew, open, boat, toe, oh, brooch, soul, low	ō	ō	ō	ō
all, Utah, taught, law, order, broad, bought	ô	ȯ	ô	ô
boil, boy	oi	ȯi	oi	oi
house, bough, now	ou	au̇	ou	ou
cup, happy	p	p	p	p
run, rhythm, carry	r	r	r	r
cent, say, scent, schism, miss	s	s	s	s
ocean, machine, special, sure, schist, conscience, nauseous, pshaw, she, tension, issue, mission, nation	sh	sh	sh	sh‿
stopped, bought, tell, Thomas, button	t	t	t	t
thin	th	th	th	th‿
then, breathe	ŦH	th	th	th́
come, does, flood, trouble, cup	u	ə	ŭ	u
beauty, feud, queue, few, adieu, view, use	ū	yü	yo͞o	yo͞o
wolf, good, should, full	u̇	u	o͝o	o͝o
maneuver, threw, move, shoe, food, you, rule, fruit	ü	ü	o͞o	o͞o
of, Stephen, very, flivver	v	v	v	v
choir, quick, will	w	w	w	w
opinion, hallelujah, you	y	y	y	y
has, discern, scissors, Xerxes, zero, buzz	z	z	z	z
garage, measure, division, azure, brazier	zh	zh	zh	zh‿

alone, fountain, moment,
pencil, complete, cautious,
circus   ə   ə   ə   ə

ITA-Initial Teaching Alphabet

æ	b	c	d	ɛɛ
face	bed	cat	dog	key
f	g	h	ie	j	k
feet	leg	hat	fly	jug	key
l	m	n	œ	p	ɼ
letter	man	nest	over	pen	girl
r	s	t	ue	v	w
red	spoon	tree	use	voice	window
y	z	ʒ	wh	ᴄh
yes	zebra	daisy	when	chair
th	ᵵh	ʃh	3	ŋ
three	the	shop	television	ring
ɑ	au	a	e	i	o
father	ball	cap	egg	milk	box
u	ω	ꞷ	ou	oi
up	book	spoon	out	oil

"ie nœ!" sed polly.

"mᴇᴇ, tꙍ!" sed molly.

"tæk them tꙍ ᴛhe siᴦcus!" cried jack.

and ᴛhat's just whot happend.

DMS—Diacritical Marking System

SHORT VOWELS & REGULAR CONSONANTS (no marks)				
A applé	F fish	K kittén	P penny	U umbrellá
B Bill	G gírl	L Lindá	Q quēēn (qu)	V valéntiné
C cŏŏkíés	H hat	M midnigh't	R Rickéy	W window
D Daddy	I Indian	N nest	S saw	X box (ks)
E egg	J jar	O ox	T tablé	Y baby
				Z zēbrá

LONG VOWELS (bar over)				
Ā apron	Ē ēar	Ī icé creám	Ō Ōćéán	Ū United States

SCHWA (comma over)		
Á ago =	É énóugh = òthér	

LETTER Y: y in yes (consonant)   ý in mý (long vowel)   funny (Note y = E not marked)

DIPHTHONGS (underline both)			
OI boil	OY boy =	OU out =	OW owl

BROAD O(A) (circumflex)			
Âll awful	Â âuto =	lông	ôr

LONG AND SHORT OO (one and two dots)	
One Dot U or Short OO Ú put	Ö gòòd
Two Dot U or Long OO Ü Jüné	Ö roóm Ë nëw

R-CONTROLLED VOWELS (underline)

far vāry fu'r he'r fu'r (r acts as vowel)

DIGRAPHS (underline)

| SH shoe | CH chair | WH which | TH that (voiced) |
| TH thing (unvoiced) | NG sing | PH =f phone | |

SECOND SOUNDS OF CONSONANTS (underline)

C c	(s) cent
S s	(z) is
G g	(j) gem

SILENT (slash)

come right he'r

EXCEPTIONS

(+over) women (+?) action

Here is a sample of a text marked with the DMS:

"Look at our fish," said Bill.

"He wants something.

But look at this box!"

Four Different Foreign Alphabets

Arabic

The different forms in the four numbered columns are used when the letters are (1) in isolation; (2) in juncture with a previous letter; (3) in juncture with the letters on both sides; (4) in juncture with a following letter.

Long vowels are represented by the consonant signs 'alif (for ā), wāw (for ū), and yā (for ī). Short vowels are not usually written.

Transliterations with subscript dots represent "emphatic" or pharyngeal consonants, which are pronounced in the usual way except that the pharynx is tightly narrowed during articulation.

ARABIC

Forms 1	2	3	4	Name	Sound
ا	ا			'alif	'
ب	ب	ـبـ	بـ	bā	b
ت	ت	ـتـ	تـ	tā	t
ث	ث	ـثـ	ثـ	thā	th
ج	ج	ـجـ	جـ	jīm	j
ح	ح	ـحـ	حـ	ḥā	ḥ
خ	خ	ـخـ	خـ	khā	kh
د	د			dāl	d
ذ	ذ			dhāl	dh
ر	ر			rā	r
ز	ز			zāy	z
س	س	ـسـ	سـ	sīn	s
ش	ش	ـشـ	شـ	shīn	sh
ص	ص	ـصـ	صـ	ṣād	ṣ
ض	ض	ـضـ	ضـ	ḍād	ḍ
ط	ط	ـطـ	طـ	ṭā	ṭ
ظ	ظ	ـظـ	ظـ	ẓā	ẓ
ع	ع	ـعـ	عـ	'ayn	'
غ	غ	ـغـ	غـ	ghayn	gh
ف	ف	ـفـ	فـ	fā	f
ق	ق	ـقـ	قـ	qāf	q
ك	ك	ـكـ	كـ	kāf	k
ل	ل	ـلـ	لـ	lām	l
م	م	ـمـ	مـ	mīm	m
ن	ن	ـنـ	نـ	nūn	n
ه	ه	ـهـ	هـ	hā	h
و	و			wāw	w
ى	ى	ـيـ	يـ	yā	y

"*The Reading Teacher's Book of Lists,* © 1984 Prentice-Hall, Inc., Englewood Cliffs, NJ 07632. By E. Fry, J. Polk, and D. Fountoukidis."

Hebrew

Vowels are not represented in normal Hebrew writing, but for educational purposes they are indicated by a system of subscript and superscript dots.

The transliterations shown in parentheses apply when the letter falls at the end of a word. The transliterations with subscript dots are pharyngeal consonants, as in Arabic.

The second forms shown are used when the letter falls at the end of a word.

Greek

The superscript ' on an initial vowel or *rhō*, called the "rough breathing," represents an aspirate. Lack of aspiration on an initial vowel is indicated by the superscript ', called the "smooth breathing."

When *gamma* precedes *kappa, xi, khi,* or another *gamma,* it has the value n and is so transliterated. The second lower-case form of *sigma* is used only in final position.

Russian

[1] This letter, called *tvordiĭ znak,* "hard sign," is very rare in modern Russian. It indicates that the previous consonant remains hard even though followed by a front vowel.

[2] This letter, called *myakiĭ znak,* "soft sign," indicates that the previous consonant is palatalized even when a front vowel does not follow.

HEBREW

Forms	Name	Sound
א	'aleph	
ב	bĕth	b (bh)
ג	gimel	g (gh)
ד	dāleth	d (dh)
ה	hē	h
ו	waw	w
ז	zayin	z
ח	ḥeth	ḥ
ט	ṭeth	ṭ
י	yodh	y
כ ך	kāph	k (kh)
ל	lāmedh	l
מ ם	mēm	m
נ ן	nūn	n
ס	samekh	s
ע	'ayin	'
פ ף	pē	p (ph)
צ ץ	ṣadhe	ṣ
ק	qōph	q
ר	rēsh	r
שׂ	sin	s
שׁ	shin	sh
ת	tāw	t (th)

GREEK

Forms	Name	Sound
A α	alpha	a.
B β	beta	b
Γ γ	gamma	g (n)
Δ δ	delta	d
E ε	epsilon	e
Z ζ	zēta	z
H η	ēta	ē
Θ θ	thēta	th
I ι	iota	i
K κ	kappa	k
Λ λ	lambda	l
M μ	mu	m
N ν	nu	n
Ξ ξ	xi	x
O o	omicron	o
Π π	pi	p
P ρ	rhō	r (rh)
Σ σ ς	sigma	s
T τ	tau	t
Υ υ	upsilon	u
Φ φ	phi	ph
X χ	khi	kh
Ψ ψ	psi	ps
Ω ω	ōmega	ō

RUSSIAN

Forms	Sound
А а	a
Б б	b
В в	v
Г г	g
Д д	d
Е е	e
Ж ж	zh
З з	z
И и Й й	i, ĭ
К к	k
Л л	l
М м	m
Н н	n
О о	o
П п	p
Р р	r
С с	s
Т т	t
У у	u
Ф ф	f
Х х	kh
Ц ц	ts
Ч ч	ch
Ш ш	sh
Щ щ	shch
Ъ ъ	"1
Ы ы	y
Ь ь	'2
Э э	e
Ю ю	yu
Я я	ya

Manual Alphabet

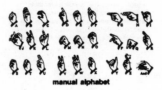

manual alphabet

Morse Code

A	.—	V	...—
B	—...	W	.——
C	—.—.	X	—..—
D	—..	Y	—.——
E	.	Z	——..
F	..—.	Á	.—.—.
G	——.	Ä	.—.—
H	....	É	..—..
I	..	Ñ	——.——
J	.———	Ö	———.
K	—.—	Ü	..——
L	.—..	1	.————
M	——	2	..———
N	—.	3	...——
O	———	4	....—
P	.——.	5	.....
Q	——.—	6	—....
R	.—.	7	——...
S	...	8	———..
T	—	9	————.
U	..—	0	—————
, (comma)	—.—.——		
. (period)	.—.—.—		
?	..——..		
;	—.—.—.		
:	———...		
/	—..—.		
- (hyphen)	—....—		
apostrophe	.————.		
parenthesis	—.——.—		
underline	..——.—		

Morse code

HOW TO COMMUNICATE WITHOUT AN ALPHABET

Alphabets represent speech sounds; symbols, on the other hand, stand directly for concepts. The concept, of course, also may be expressed in the form of a word or several words that use the alphabet.

The first list in this section is a general list of symbols. In looking over the symbols, you will see that they tend to fall into subject categories, such as mathematics, weather, astronomy, and diacritical marks. Many specialized fields have sets of symbols or abbreviations, such as pharmacy, chemistry, physics, computer programming, and engineering. Hence, some sets of symbols are best learned in conjunction with the study of that particular subject. However, all students must know that many symbols such as these can be found in dictionaries, and they should know what some of the more common ones mean.

We might have taken our alphabet from the Romans but, thankfully, we did not take their number system. Most of the time we use the Arabic numeral system, but on some formal occasions we do use Roman numerals. Students should be at least familiar enough with the Roman numerals to write a date and to puzzle out the dates inscribed on the cornerstones of many buildings.

Helping students develop essays, short stories, term papers, or other writing goes more smoothly when you use proofreading symbols. Introduce these early in the school year and use them throughout. The time and space saved may be devoted to comments on content and encouragement.

General Signs and Symbols

+ plus	∟ right angle	≦ or ≤ less than or equal to	∴ therefore
− minus	△ triangle		∵ because
± plus or minus	□ square			absolute value	‾ vinculum (above letter)
∓ minus or plus	▭ rectangle	∪ logical sum or union	( ) parentheses
× multiplied by	▱ parallelogram	∩ logical product or intersection	[ ] brackets
÷ divided by	○ circle		{ } braces
= equal to	⌒ arc of circle	⊂ is contained in	° degree
≠ or ≠ not equal to	⊥ equilateral	ε is a member of; permittivity; mean error	′ minute
≈ or ≑ nearly equal to	≙ equiangular	: is to; ratio	″ second
≡ identical with	√ radical; root; square root	∷ as; proportion	△ increment
≢ not identical with	∛ cube root	≐ approaches	ω angular frequency; solid angle
⇌ equivalent	∜ fourth root	→ approaches limit of	Ω ohm
∼ difference	Σ sum	∝ varies as	μΩ microhm
≅ congruent to	! or ∟ factorial product	‖ parallel	MΩ megohm
> greater than	∞ infinity	⊥ perpendicular	Φ magnetic flux
≯ not greater than	∫ integral	∠ angle	
< less than	ƒ function		
≮ not less than	∂ or δ differential; variation		
≧ or ≥ greater than or equal to	π pi		

℥	ounce	@	at	℔	per	`	grave
ʒ	dram	*	asterisk	#	number	~	tilde
℈	scruple	†	dagger	/	virgule; slash; solidus; shilling	^	circumflex
f℥	fluid ounce	‡	double dagger	©	copyright	¯	macron
fʒ	fluid dram	§	section	%	per cent	˘	breve
♏	minim	☞	index	℅	care of	¨	dieresis
& or &	and; ampersand	´	acute	%	account of	.	cedilla
						∧	caret

Ψ	dielectric flux; electrostatic flux	♓	Pisces	♀	Venus	∞	haze; dust haze
ρ	resistivity	♂	conjunction	⊖ or ⊕	Earth	T	thunder
Λ	equivalent conductivity	♉	opposition	♂	Mars	<	sheet lightning
ℛ	reluctance	△	trine	♃	Jupiter	⦵	solar corona
→	direction of flow	□	quadrature	♄	Saturn	⊕	solar halo
⇌	electric current	*	sextile	♅	Uranus	⧖	thunderstorm
◯	benzene ring	☊	dragon's head, ascending node	Ψ	Neptune	＼	direction
→	yields	☋	dragon's tail, descending node	♇	Pluto	○ or ⊙ or ①	annual
⇌	reversible reaction			♈	Aries	⊙⊙ or ②	biennial
↓	precipitate	●	rain	♉	Taurus	♃	perennial
↑	gas	*	snow	♊	Gemini	♂ or ♂	male
⁰/₀₀	salinity	⊠	snow on ground	♋	Cancer	♀	female
☉ or ☼	sun	—	floating ice crystals	♌	Leo	□	male (in charts)
● or ●	new moon	▲	hail	♍	Virgo	○	female (in charts)
☽	first quarter	△	sleet	♎	Libra	℞	take (from Latin *Recipe*)
○ or ⊗	full moon	V	frostwork	♏	Scorpius	ĀĀ or Ā or āā	of each (doctor's prescription)
☾	last quarter	⊔	hoarfrost	♐	Sagittarius		
☿	Mercury	≡	fog	♑	Capricornus	℔	pound
				♒	Aquarius		

Proofreading Symbols

Notation in Margin	How Indicated in Copy	Explanation
¶	true.∧The best rule to follow	New paragraph
⌒	living room	Close up
#	Mary had a	Insert space
⁀	Mary had a lamb little.	Transpose
sp	There were ⑤ children	Spell out
cap	mary had a little lamb.	Capitalize
lc	Mary had a little Lamb.	Lower case
℔	The correct procedure	Delete or take out
stet	Mary had a little lamb.	Restore crossed-out word(s)
little	Mary had a ∧ lamb.	Insert word(s) in margin

Roman Numerals

Roman	Arabic	Roman	Arabic
I	1	XX	20
II	2	XXI	21
III	3	XXIX	29
IV	4	XXX	30
V	5	XL	40
VI	6	XLVIII	48
VII	7	IL	49
VIII	8	L	50
IX	9	LX	60
X	10	XC	90
XI	11	XCVIII	98
XII	12	IC	99
XIII	13	C	100
XIV	14	CI	101
XV	15	CC	200
XVI	16	D	500
XVII	17	DC	600
XVIII	18	CM	900
XIX	19	M	1,000
		MCMLXXXIV	1984

OTHER USEFUL LISTS

The following lists have only one thing in common: They are useful.

The first outlines the general classification systems used by libraries. Most universities, research organizations, large public libraries, and, of course, the Library of Congress, use the Library of Congress System. Most school libraries and smaller public libraries use the Dewey Decimal System for classifying books and other materials. Students should have at least a modest acquaintance with both systems. To develop familiarity, give the students both lists and ask them to classify different book titles by both systems. A better, more realistic lesson is to take them to the library and have them use the systems to find real books for research projects, class use, or recreational reading.

Foreign words and phrases are used in many novels, magazine and newspaper articles, and some academic writing. Your students might enjoy learning some of the more common ones. They also can pick them out in speech and reading assignments. Some students will demonstrate a penchant for using foreign phrases in their ordinary speech to impress their friends.

Nonsexist language has had an impact in areas beyond the ERA, the women's movement, and activist associations. It has become the standard in the business and academic worlds. Textbooks are being written that show an increasing awareness of and sensitivity to bias and sexism. You might call your students' attention to sexist language in their own writing. They could make half the world angry.

Library Classification Systems

Library of Congress Classification

		P	Language and Literature
A	General Works	PA	Classical Language and Literature
B	Philosophy and Religion		
C	History of Civilization	PB–PH	Modern European Languages
D	General History		
E–F	History–Americas	PJ–PL	Oriental Language and Literature
G	Geography and Anthropology	PN	General Literature
H	Social Sciences	PQ	French, Italian, Spanish, Portuguese Literature
J	Political Science		
K	Law	PR	English Literature
L	Education	PS	American Literature
M	Music	PT	German, Dutch, Scandinavian Literature
N	Fine Arts		

Library of Congress Classification cont.

Q	Science	U	Military Science
R	Medicine	V	Naval Science
S	Agriculture	Z	Bibliography
T	Technology		

Simplifed Dewey Decimal System

000	General Works	400	Philology
100	Philosophy and Psychology	500	Pure Science
200	Religion	600	Applied Science
300	Social Sciences	700	Fine Arts
310	Statistics	800	Literature
320	Political Science	900	History
330	Economics		
331	Labor Economics		
331.3	Labor by Age Groups		
331.39	Employed Middle Aged and Aged		
340	Law		
350	Administration		
360	Welfare and Social Institutions		
370	Education		
380	Public Services and Utilities		
390	Customs and Folklore		

Foreign Words and Phrases

addenda—list of additions (Latin)

ad hoc—with respect to this condition (Latin)

ad infinitum—to infinity (Latin)

ad nauseam—to the point of disgust (Latin)

à la carte—according to the menu (French)

à la mode—in fashion (French)

alfresco—outdoors (Italian)

au contraire—on the contrary (French)

au revoir—until we meet again (French)

à votre sante—to your health (French)

bona fide—in good faith (Latin)

bon jour—good day (French)

bon soir—good evening (French)

bon vivant—lover of good living (French)

bon voyage—have a good voyage (French)

caveat emptor—let the buyer beware (Latin)

circa—about (Latin)

cogito ergo sum—I think, therefore I am (Latin)

coup d'etat—quick political change (French)

cul-de-sac—dead end (French)

de rigueur—required (French)

double entendre—double meaning (French)

emeritus—retired after long service (Latin)

en masse—in a large group (French)

en route—on the way (French)

entourage—those closely associated with a person (French)

e pluribus unum—one from many (Latin)

errata—list of errors (Latin)

esprit de corps—group spirit (French)

et cetera—and others (Latin)

eureka—I have found it (Latin)

faux pas—mistakes (French)

hors d'oeuvre—appetizer (French)

in memoriam—in memory of (Latin)

in re—regarding (Latin)

in toto—totally (Latin)

je ne sais quoi—I don't know what (French)

laissez faire—noninterference (French)

mâitre d'hôtel—head waiter (French)

malapropos—out of place (French)

mañana—tomorrow (Spanish)

mardi gras—Shrove Tuesday (French)

mea culpa—my fault (Latin)

modus operandi—manner of working (Latin)

nee—born (French)

n'est'ce pas?—isn't that so? (French)

noblesse oblige—rank imposes obligations (French)

Noel—Christmas (Latin)

nom de plume—pen name (French)

non sequitur—it does not follow (Latin)

nota bene—note well (Latin)

"The Reading Teacher's Book of Lists, © 1984 Prentice-Hall, Inc., Englewood Cliffs, NJ 07632. By E. Fry, J. Polk, and D. Fountoukidis."

nuance—subtle distinction (French)
pardonnez-moi—excuse me (French)
penchant—strong liking or inclination (French)
persona non grata—person not accepted (Latin)
per—for (Latin)
pièce de resistance—the irresistible part (French)
prima dona—first lady (Italian)
pro forma—done as a matter of formality (Latin)
pro rata—according to a rate or proportion (Latin)
protégé—one under the guidance of another (French)
quid pro quo—one thing for another (Latin)
raconteur—story teller (French)
raison d'être—reason for existence (French)
résumé—summary (French)
savoir faire—social know-how (French)
sine qua non—indispensable (Latin)
status quo—the way things are (Latin)
stet—leave as is (Latin)
sub rosa—secret or confidential (Latin)
tempus fugit—time flies (Latin)
tout de suite—immediately (French)
vice versa—conversely (Latin)
voilà—there it is (French)
Wanderlust—passion for traveling (German)

Guidelines for Nonsexist Language

Slanted	Unbiased	Comment
The student chooses his assignments in this class.	The student chooses the assignments in this class.	omit *his*
	Students choose their assignments in this class.	change to plural
	The assignments in this class are chosen by the students.	rephrase
Man's search for knowledge has led him	The search for knowledge has led us	rephrased using first person

into areas unknown 50 years ago.	into areas unknown 50 years ago.	
man, mankind	people, humanity, human beings, humankind, the human species, the average person	use inclusive group
manpower	workers, personnel, staff, employees	use inclusive group
Each participant is to bring his own equipment.	Each participant is to bring his or her own equipment.	use *his or her*
The boys finally let Amy play on their team.	The boys finally "let" Amy play on their team.	shows bias of the team, not the author
The teacher should be on time for her class.	Teachers should be on time for their classes.	omit stereotype and make plural
This child suffers from lack of mothering.	This child suffers from lack of nurturing. This child suffers from lack of parenting.	inclusive noun substituted
The chairman of the committee recommends this book.	The chairperson recommends this book.	use nonspecific noun
chairman of the meeting	moderator, leader, discussion leader	use nonspecific noun
Dear Sir	Dear Editor	use nonspecific noun
	Dear Sir or Madam	use both or inclusive noun

V
TESTING

YOU CAN'T GET OUT OF TESTING!

Three things are certain in this world: death, taxes, and taking tests. This section will help you prepare students for taking tests. First are some directions —not the kind of directions the test makers tell the testees but the kind of directions you should teach your students long before and just before taking any test.

We also present a good list of the kinds of words used on tests. If students pay very careful attention to these words, their chances of making an error will be greatly diminished. This is a group of words no student can survive well without. They are key words and terms needed in taking an examination or in following directions in a workbook, worksheet, or other teaching materials.

If you *underline* when you are supposed to *circle,* or *compare* when you are supposed to *contrast,* your grade could be lowered considerably.

All students need to have these words pointed out to them. They begin using them in first grade with worksheets, and continue using them for college entrance examinations.

They perhaps are taught most effectively in context. Every time you give students a test or a written exercise, point out these test words. Special lessons on these words can also be effective. They are an important part of "testwiseness" or "studentship."

Words Used on Standardized Tests and Workbook Exercises (for younger students)

answer sheet	definition	name	reason
best	directions	next	rhyming
blank	does not belong	none of these	right
booklet	end	not true	row
check your work	error	opposite	same as
choose	example	pairs	sample
circle	finish	paragraph	section
column	following	passage	second
compare	go on to next page	print	stop
complete	item	probably	true
contrast	mark	put an X	underline
correct	match	question	wait for directions
cross out	missing	read	

Important Modifiers that Can Affect Test Scores

all	best	few	less	most	often	sometimes
always	every	good	many	never	seldom	usually
bad	equal	invariably	more	non	some	worst

(Also see the Signal Words in section VI.)

Key Words and Phrases for Use in Essay Exams
(for older students)

analyze	define	formulate	predict	solve
apply	demonstrate	generate	propose	specify
argue	describe	generalize	prove	state
assess	develop	give an example of	provide	suggest
categorize	diagram	identify	rank	summarize
cause	differentiate	illustrate	react	support
cite evidence	discuss	interpret	reason	survey
classify	distinguish	justify	recall	tell
compare	draw conclusions	list	recommend	trace
construct	effect	mention	relate	utilize
contrast	enumerate	organize	relationship	why
convince	estimate	outline	select	
create	evaluate	paraphrase	show how	
criticize	explain	point out	significance	

Strategies Used in Taking Tests

General

- If you have a choice of seats, try to sit in a place where you will be least disturbed (e.g., not by a door).
- When you first receive the test, glance over it, noting the types of questions and the number of points to be awarded for them.
- Budget your time, making sure you allow sufficient time for the questions that are worth the most points.
- Read directions carefully. Underline important direction words, such as *choose one, briefly,* and so on.
- Start with the questions that are easiest.

"The Reading Teacher's Book of Lists, © 1984 Prentice-Hall, Inc., Englewood Cliffs, NJ 07632. By E. Fry, J. Polk, and D. Fountoukidis."

- Be alert for information in some questions that may provide help with other more difficult questions. If you find such information, be sure to note it before you forget.

Objective Tests

- Before you start, find out if there is a penalty for guessing and if you can choose more than one answer.
- Read the questions and all possible answers carefully.
- Be especially careful about questions with the choices *all of the above* and *none of the above.*
- Underline key words and qualifiers such as *never, always,* and so on.
- Answer all of the questions you know first.
- Make a mark next to those you can't answer so you can go back to them later.
- After you complete the questions you know, go back and reread the ones you didn't answer the first time.
- If you still can't answer a question the second time through, here are some strategies to try:

1. For a multiple choice item, read the question; then stop and try to think of an answer. Look to see if one of the choices is similar to your answer.
2. Start by eliminating those answers that you know are not correct and then choose among the remaining alternatives.
3. Read through all of the answers very carefully, and then go back to the question. Sometimes you can pick up clues just by thinking about the different answers you have been given to choose from.
4. Try paraphrasing the question and then recalling some examples.
5. For a multiple choice item, try reading the question separately with each alternative answer.

- If there is no penalty for guessing, make sure you answer all questions, even if you have to guess blindly.
- If there is a penalty for guessing, you usually should guess if you can eliminate one of the choices.
- If you have time, check over the exam. Change an answer only if you can think of a good reason to do so. Generally you're better off if you stick with your first choice.

"The Reading Teacher's Book of Lists, © 1984 Prentice-Hall, Inc., Englewood Cliffs, NJ 07632. By E. Fry, J. Polk, and D. Fountoukidis."

Essay Tests

- Read through all of the questions carefully.
- Mark the important direction words that tell you what you're to do: *compare, trace, list,* and so on.
- Number the parts of the question so you don't forget to answer all of them.
- Take time to try to understand what the question is asking. Don't jump to conclusions on the basis of a familiar word or two.
- As you read through the questions, briefly jot down ideas that come into your mind.
- Briefly outline your answers before you begin to write. Refer back to the question to be sure your answer is focused on the question.
- As you write, be careful to stick to your outline.
- If possible, allow generous margins so you can add information later if you need to.
- Don't spend so much time on one question that you don't have time for other questions.
- If you have time, proofread what you have written. This is a good time to double-check to make sure you have answered all of the parts of the question.
- If you run short of time, quickly outline answers to the questions that remain. List the information without worrying about complete sentences.

Quantitative Tests

- Read the questions carefully to make sure you understand what is being asked.
- Do the questions you are sure of first.
- Budget your time to allow for questions worth the most points.
- Don't just write answers. Make sure to show your work.
- As you work out answers try to do it neatly and to write down each step. This helps you avoid careless mistakes and makes it possible for the tester to follow your work. It may make the difference between partial credit and no credit for a wrong answer.
- Check your answer when you finish to make sure it makes sense. If it doesn't seem logical, check again.

- If you are missing information needed to calculate an answer, check to see if it was given in a previous problem or if you can compute it in some way.

- Check to see if you have used all of the information provided. You may not always need to, but you should double-check to be sure.

- If you have time, go back and check your calculations.

THE CLOZE TECHNIQUE

The *cloze technique* is simply a sentence completion technique in which a word (or part of a word or several words) is omitted and the student fills in the omitted part.

This is used as a test of reading comprehension or language ability, a reading comprehension or language teaching drill, a research tool, or a readability measure or estimate of passage difficulty.*

Cloze passages can be made on any subject or any type of material very easily by the teacher. All you need to do is omit parts of the passage and ask the students to fill in the missing parts. The following list presents some of the possible variations.

Cloze Variations

Mechanical Deletion Variations

1. Vary every *n*th word (5th, 10th, etc.). (This is the traditional cloze method.)

2. Randomized (average every *n*th word).

Selective Deletion Variations

1. Structure words or content words only.

2. Only one part of speech.

3. Only words that best fit a particular comprehension skill objective.

Answer Variations

1. Exact word answers vs. synonym answers. (You can permit either.)

2. Written versus oral answers.

3. Completion (fill in blank).

4. Multiple choice (sometimes called *Maze*; student is given a choice of three answers).

5. Vary multiple-choice deflectors (wrong choices).

   a. similar visual word form of phonic sound. Example: *pen-Ben*

   b. similar part of speech

   c. similar meaning

---

*To estimate suitable readability or difficulty level of a passage, one suggested criterion is that a student should be able to fill in 35 percent to 44 percent of the exact missing words when every fifth word is deleted from a 250-word passage. This gives an instructional level.

"The Reading Teacher's Book of Lists, © 1984 Prentice-Hall, Inc., Englewood Cliffs, NJ 07632. By E. Fry, J. Polk, and D. Fountoukidis."

6. Self-correction, teacher correction, other student correction.

7. Discuss answers versus no discussion.

8. Correct spelling required.

Size of Deletion Variations
One word, two words, phrase, one letter, two letters, and so on.

Passage Content Variations
Prose, science, history, and so on.

Readability Level Variations
1. First grade, second grade, and so on.

2. Imageability of difficulty.

3. Legibility.

Passage Length Variations
1. Sentence.

2. Paragraph.

3. 500 words.

   and so on.

Preparation Variations
1. Student reads complete (no blanks) passage before answering.

2. Student doesn't read complete (no blanks) passage before answering.

3. Teacher has preparation lesson, like DRA, before answering.

4. Student is told to guess.

Cueing Variations
1. None. (This is the traditional method.)

2. First letter of answer given.

3. Part of word deleted: blend, bound morpheme, prefix, suffix, root, vowels, consonants.

Listening Variations
1. Complete passage is read to students before silent cloze written drill.

2. Cloze drill done orally. (Teacher reads drill aloud, student answers orally.)

WHAT DO TEST SCORES MEAN?

Most school districts give tests. Most teachers get the results of those tests. What do these test scores mean? How do you interpret them? One place to start is with an understanding of the terminology that test makers use. Familiarity with terms like *grade equivalent, percentile rank,* and *stanine* also helps you explain test results to interested and sometimes anxious students and parents.

Incidentally, a handy little notion to keep in mind when considering a student's placement and progress is the Chronological Age Grade Placement. To get this, just subtract 5.4 (the average age at which children enter school) from the student's current age. Stated more formally, chronological age − 5.4 = chronological age grade placement (CA − 5.4 = CAGP). For example, ask a student how old he or she is. If the answer is, "I'm ten years old and my birthday was six months ago," subtract 5.4 from 10.5, and the CAGP or expected grade placement based on age is 5.1. That is, the student should be in the fifth grade, and if his or her intellectual ability (IQ) is normal, he or she should be reading at a beginning fifth-grade level. For younger children, you would expect lower reading scores, just because of age. This helps you to keep a proper perspective, especially when considering students who are the youngest in your class.

Testing Terms

Achievement tests—Tests that measure how much students have learned in a particular subject area.

Aptitude tests—Tests that attempt to predict how well students will do in learning new subject matter in the future.

CEEB test scores—College Entrance Examination Board test scores. This type of score is used by exams such as the Scholastic Aptitude Test. It has a mean of 500 and a standard deviation of 100.

Correlation coefficient—A measure of the strength and direction (positive or negative) of the relationship between two things.

Criterion-referenced tests—Tests where the performance of the test taker is compared with a fixed standard or criterion. The primary purpose is to determine if the test taker has mastered a particular unit sufficiently to proceed to the next unit.

Diagnostic tests—Tests that are used to identify individual students' strengths and weaknesses in a particular subject area.

Grade equivalent scores—The grade level for which a score is the real or estimated average. For example, a grade equivalent score of 3.5 is the average score of students halfway through the third grade.

Mean—The arithmetic average of a group of scores.

Median—The middle score in a group of scores.

Mode—The score that was obtained by the largest number of test takers.

Normal distribution—A bell-shaped distribution of test scores where scores are distributed symmetrically around the mean and where the mean, median, and mode are the same.

"The Reading Teacher's Book of Lists, © 1984 Prentice-Hall, Inc., Englewood Cliffs, NJ 07632. By E. Fry, J. Polk, and D. Fountoukidis."

Norming population—The group of people to whom the test was administered in order to establish performance standards for various age or grade levels. When the norming population is composed of students from various sections of the country, the resulting standards are called *national norms*. When the norming population is drawn from a local school or school district, the standards are referred to as *local norms*.

Norm-referenced tests—Tests for which the results of the test taker are compared with the performance of others (the norming population) who have taken the test.

Percentile rank—A comparison of an individual's raw score with the raw score of others who took the test (usually this is a comparison with the norming population). This comparison tells the test taker the percentage of other test takers whose scores fall below his or her own score.

Raw score—The initial score assigned to test performance. This score usually is the number correct; however, sometimes it may include a correction for guessing.

Reliability—A measure of the extent to which a test is consistent in measuring whatever it purports to measure. Reliability coefficients range from 0 to 1. In order to be considered highly reliable a test should have a reliability coefficient of 0.90 or above. There are several types of reliability coefficients: *parallel-form* reliability (the correlation of two different forms of a test), *test-retest* reliability (the correlation of test scores from two different administrations of the same test to the same population), *split-half* reliability (the correlation between two halves of the same test), and *internal consistency* reliability (a reliability coefficient computed using a Kuder-Richardson formula).

Standard deviation—A measure of the variability of test scores. If most scores are close to the mean, the standard deviation will be small. If the scores have a wide range, then the standard deviation will be large.

Standard error of measurement (SEM)—An estimate of the amount of measurement error in a test. This provides an estimate of how much a person's actual test score may vary from his or her hypothetical true score. The larger the SEM, the less confidence can be placed in the score as a reflection of an individual's true ability.

Standardized tests—Tests that have been given to groups of students under standardized conditions and for which norms have been established.

Stanine scores—Whole number scores between 1 and 9 which have a mean of 5 and a standard deviation of 2.

True score—The score that would be obtained on a given test if that test were perfectly reliable. This is a hypothetical score.

Validity—The extent to which a test measures what it is supposed to measure. Two common types of validity are *content validity* (the extent to which the content of the test covers situations and subject matter about which conclusions will be drawn) and *predictive validity* (the extent to which predictions made from the test are confirmed by evidence gathered at some later time).

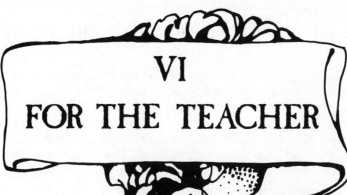

VI
FOR THE TEACHER

SOME TEACHING TRICKS OF THE TRADE

A list of ten games appears first in this section because games can be used in teaching so many areas covered in other parts of this book. They are adaptable for most of the word lists, such as the Instant Words, Math Terms, or Contractions.

The 100 Ways to Praise has some old, tried and true praise statements and a few you probably haven't thought of. Use a few more of these, and school will be a more pleasant place, where motivation for learning will take a dramatic upswing. Be free with praise for even minor successes; it will encourage larger successes. One student we remember needed positive feedback for learning even one new thing in a whole session. Take care, however, never to be phony and praise when it isn't deserved; you will lose your credibility and the value of future praise.

The Readability Graph is included so you will have it on hand when you need it. Use it to help judge the difficulty level (in grade level scores) of the materials your students use so you can better match the reading selection to the students' reading abilities.

We aren't going to suggest that you have the students write book reports. Teachers always know how to do that. Instead, we have a list of 40 things your students can do instead of writing a book report.

Signal words serve a unique purpose in language. They are words put into the passage by the author to tell the reader how to read. They tell the reader things like, "I am going to give you a sequence of ideas," or, "Watch out, the end is coming up and this last point might be especially important." This list of signal words is certainly incomplete; in fact, the whole idea of signal words is a bit nebulous. However, it is interesting and potentially quite important for the reading teacher and those many students trying to comprehend better.

Take the signal words one group at a time, and show them to your students. Get the students to add more words in the same category. If you concentrate on one type of signal for a few days, students can add words as they come across them in their daily reading. The growing signal word list can be kept on the chalkboard for several days and in individual student notebooks.

Propaganda is a rather harsh term applied to relatively familiar material. If you like the material, you might call them *persuasion devices*. Whatever you call them, students should learn to recognize them. A great lesson is to have students bring in samples of newspaper ads or political speeches to place on the bulletin board and analyze the techniques used in them.

Study skills are included here for two reasons. First, the area of study skills seems to be a bit fuzzy. By looking over skills that usually are associated with this area we can get a better idea of what it is. Second, these skills are important not only to consider but also to develop—beginning in elementary school and working up through high school. Be sure to integrate these into your lessons regularly. Don't just present them all at once in a single study unit.

Ten Basic Teaching Games and Teaching Situations

Use these games or activities, or others that you like, for teaching the word lists in this book.

1. **Pairs**. A card game for two to five players. Five cards are dealt to each player, and the remainder of the deck is placed in the center of the table. The object of the game is to get as many pairs as possible. There are only two cards alike in each deck. To play, the player to the right of the dealer may ask any other player if he or she has a specific card. For example, "Do you have *and*?" The player asking must hold the mate in his or her hand. The player who is asked must give up the card if he or she holds it. If the first player does not get the card asked for, he or she draws one card from the pile. Then the next player has a turn at asking for a card.

   If the player succeeds in getting the card asked for, either from another player or from the pile, he or she gets another turn. As soon as the player gets a pair, he or she puts the pair down in front of him or her. The player with the most pairs at the end of the game wins.
   Note: A deck of 50 cards (25 pairs) is good for two to five players.

2. **Bingo**. Played like regular Bingo except that the players' boards have 25 words in place of numbers. Children can use bits of paper for markers and the caller can randomly call off words from a list. Be certain when making the boards that the words are arranged in a different order on each card.

the	of	it	with	at
a	can	on	are	this
is	will	you	to	and
your	that	we	as	but
be	in	not	for	have

3. **Board Games.** Trace a path on posterboard. Mark off one-inch spaces. Write a word in each space. Students advance from start by tossing dice, until one reaches the finish line. Students must correctly pronounce (or give meaning or sample use) of the word in the square. Use three pennies if you don't have dice; shake and advance number of squares for heads up.

4. **Contests.** Students, individually or as teams, try to get more words in a category than anyone else. The teacher may start the contest by giving three homographs. The students try to amass the longest list of homographs. There may be a time limit.

5. **Spelling.** Use the list words in spelling lessons or have an old-fashioned spelling bee.

6. **Use Them in a Sentence.** Either orally or written. Award points for the longest, funniest, saddest, or most believable.

7. **Word Wheels.** To make a word wheel, attach an inner circle to a larger circle with a paper fastener. Turn the inner wheel to match outer parts. This is great for compound words, phonograms, or matching a word to a picture clue. Sliding strips do the same thing.

8. **Matching.** Make worksheets with two columns of words or word parts. Students draw a line from an item in column A to the item in column B that matches (*prefix* and *root*, *word* and *meaning*, two synonyms, etc.). Matching also can be done by matching two halves of a card that has been cut to form puzzle pieces.

9. **Flash Cards.** The word or word part is written on one side of a card. The teacher or tutor flashes the cards for the student to read instantly. Cards also can be shuffled and read by the student. Cards also can be used in sentence building, finding synonyms and antonyms, and so on.

10. **Hidden Words** (or Word Search Puzzle). To make a word search puzzle, write words horizontally, vertically, or diagonally on a grid (graph paper is fine), one letter per box. Fill in all the other boxes with letters at random. Students try to locate all of the target words. When they find one they circle it.

C	E	Z	O
B	A	M	D
R	S	T	O
F	M	X	G

100 Ways to Praise

Fantastic!
That's really nice.
That's clever.
You're right on target.
Thank you!
Wow!
That's great!
Very creative.
Very interesting.
I like the way you're working.
Good thinking.
That's an interesting way of looking at it.
It's a pleasure to teach you when you work like this.
Now you've figured it out.
Keep up the good work.
You've made my day.
Purrrfect!
You're on the ball today.
This is something special.
Everyone's working so hard.
That's quite an improvement.
Much better.
Keep it up.
That's the right answer.
Exactly right!

Super!
Superior work.
Great going!
Where have you been hiding all this talent?
I knew you could do it!
You're really moving.
Good job.
What neat work!
You really outdid yourself today.
That's a good point.
That's a very good observation.
That's certainly one way of looking at it.
This kind of work pleases me very much.
Congratulations! You got _____ more correct today.
That's right. Good for you.
Terrific!
I bet your parents will be proud to see the job you did on this.
That's an interesting point of view.
You're really going to town.
You've got it now.
Nice going.
You make it look so easy.
This shows you've been thinking.
You're becoming an expert at this.
Topnotch work!
This gets a four star rating.
Beautiful.
I'm very proud of the way you worked today.
Excellent work.
I appreciate your help.
Very good. Why don't you show the class?
The results were worth all your hard work.
You've come a long way with this one.
I appreciate your cooperation.
Thank you for getting right to work.
Marvelous.
I commend you for your quick thinking.
I like the way you've handled this.
That looks like it's going to be a good report.
I like the way you are working today.
My goodness, how impressive!

"The Reading Teacher's Book of Lists, © 1984 Prentice-Hall, Inc., Englewood Cliffs, NJ 07632. By E. Fry, J. Polk, and D. Fountoukidis."

You're on the right track now.
This is quite an accomplishment.
I like how you've tackled this assignment.
A powerful argument!
That's coming along nicely.
I like the way you've settled down to work.
You've shown a lot of patience with this.
I noticed that you got right down to work.
You've really been paying attention.
It looks like you've put a lot of work into this.
You've put in a full day today.
This is prize-winning work.
An A-1 paper!
I like your style.
Pulitzer-prize-winner in training.
Your style has spark.
Your work has such personality.
That's very perceptive.
This is a moving scene.
Your remark shows a lot of sensitivity.
This really has flair.
Clear, concise, and complete!
A well-developed theme!
You are really in touch with the feeling here.
This piece has pizzazz!
A splendid job!
You're right on the mark.
Good reasoning.
Very fine work.
You really scored here.
Outstanding!
This is a winner!
Go to the head of the class.
Superb!

GRAPH FOR ESTIMATING READABILITY —EXTENDED

by Edward Fry, Rutgers University Reading Center, New Brunswick, N.J. 08904

Average number of syllables per 100 words

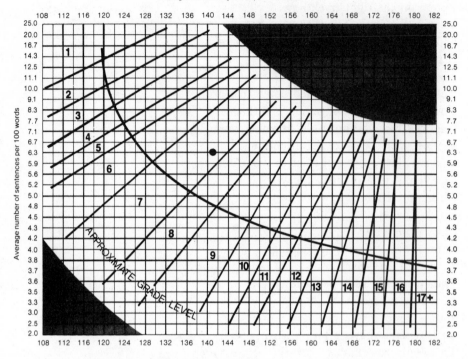

DIRECTIONS: Randomly select 3 one hundred word passages from a book or an article. Plot average number of syllables and average number of sentences per 100 words on graph to determine the grade level of the material. Choose more passages per book if great variability is observed and conclude that the book has uneven readability. Few books will fall in gray area but when they do grade level scores are invalid.

Count proper nouns, numerals and initializations as words. Count a syllable for each symbol. For example, "1945" is 1 word and 4 syllables and "IRA" is 1 word and 3 syllables.

EXAMPLE:		SYLLABLES	SENTENCES
1st Hundred Words		124	6.6
2nd Hundred Words		141	5.5
3rd Hundred Words		158	6.8
	AVERAGE	141	6.3

READABILITY 7th GRADE (see dot plotted on graph)

For further information and validity data see the Journal of Reading December, 1977.

Directions for Using Readability Graph

1. Randomly select three sample passages and count out exactly 100 words beginning with the beginning of a sentence. Do count proper nouns, initializations, and numerals.

2. Count the number of sentences in the 100 words, estimating length of the fraction of the last sentence to the nearest tenth.

3. Count the total number of syllables in the 100-word passage. If you don't have a hand counter available, an easy way is simply to put a

"The Reading Teacher's Book of Lists, © 1984 Prentice-Hall, Inc., Englewood Cliffs, NJ 07632. By E. Fry, J. Polk, and D. Fountoukidis."

mark above every syllable over one in each word. Then, when you get to the end of the passage, count the number of marks and add 100. Small calculators also can be used as counters by pushing the numeral 1; then push the plus sign for each word or syllable when counting.

4. Enter the graph with *average* sentence length and *average* number of syllables; plot the dot where the two lines intersect. The area where the dot is plotted will give you the approximate grade level.

5. If a great deal of variability is found in syllable count or sentence count, putting more samples into the average is desirable.

6. A *word* is defined as a group of symbols with a space on either side. Thus, *Joe, IRA, 1945,* and *&* are each one word.

7. A *syllable* is defined as a phonetic syllable. Generally, there are as many syllables as vowel sounds. For example, *stopped* is one syllable and *wanted* is two syllables. When counting syllables for numerals and initializations, count one syllable for each symbol. For example, *1945* is four syllables, *IRA* is three syllables, and *&* is one syllable.

40 Book Report Alternatives

1. Draw a time line to illustrate the events in the story.
2. Construct a story map to show the plot and setting.
3. Create a jacket for the book, complete with illustrations and blurbs.
4. Prepare a chart showing the characters, their relationships, and a few biographical facts about each.
5. Create a poster-sized ad for the book.
6. Have a panel discussion if several students read the same book.
7. Dramatize an incident or an important character alone or with others.
8. Do a radio announcement to publicize the book.
9. Have individual conferences with students to get their personal reactions.
10. Appoint a committee to conduct peer discussion and seminars on books.
11. Illustrate the story, take slides, coordinate music and narration, and give a multimedia presentation.
12. Write a play based on the continuation of the story or a new adventure for the characters.
13. Give a demonstration of what was learned from a how-to book.
14. Compose a telegram about the book, limited to twenty words.

15. Dramatically read a part of the book to the class to get them hooked.

16. Keep a diary of one of the characters in the story, using first person.

17. Write a letter to the author telling why you liked the book, your favorite parts, what you would have done with the plot.

18. Be a newspaper columnist, write a review for the book section.

19. Explain how the story might have ended if a key character or incident was changed.

20. Write a letter to the key character to tell him or her how to solve the problem.

21. Write a newspaper article based on an incident from the book.

22. Write a biography of the leading character, using information from the book.

23. Write an obituary article about a key character, giving an account of what he or she was best known for.

24. Give a testimonial speech citing the character for special distinctions noted in the book.

25. Compare the movie and book versions of the same story.

26. Make a diorama to show the time and setting of the story.

27. Have a character day. Dress up as your favorite character in the story and relive some of the story.

28. Rewrite the story as a TV movie, include staging directions.

29. Examine the story for the author's craft and try to write a story of your own, imitating the use of tone, setting, style, and so on.

30. Memorize your favorite lines, or write them down for future quoting.

31. Make sketches of some of the action sequences.

32. Read the story into a tape recorder so that others may listen to it.

33. Research the period of history in which the story is set.

34. Make a list of similes, metaphors, or succinct descriptions.

35. Make puppets and present a show based on the book.

36. Build a clay or papier mâché bust of a key character.

37. Give a "chalk talk" about the book.

38. Paint a mural that shows the key incidents in the story.

39. Rewrite the story for students in a lower grade. Keep it interesting.

40. File information about the book in a classroom cross-reference. Include author, story type, list of books it is similar to, and so on.

"The Reading Teacher's Book of Lists, © 1984 Prentice-Hall, Inc., Englewood Cliffs, NJ 07632. By E. Fry, J. Polk, and D. Fountoukidis."

Signal Words—Words the Author Uses to Tell the Reader How to Read

1. **Continuation signals** (Warning—there are more ideas to come):

and	also	another
again	and finally	first of all
a final reason	furthermore	in addition
last of all	likewise	more
moreover	next	one reason
other	secondly	similarly
too	with	

2. **Change-of-direction signals** (Watch out—we're doubling back):

although	but	conversely
despite	different from	even though
however	in contrast	instead of
in spite of	nevertheless	otherwise
the opposite	on the contrary	on the other hand
rather	still	yet
while	though	

3. **Sequence signals** (There is an order to these ideas):

first, second, third	A, B, C
in the first place	for one thing
then	next
before	now
after	while
into (*far into the night*)	until
last	during
since	always
o'clock	on time
later	earlier

4. **Illustration signals** (Here's what that principle means in reality):

for example	specifically
for instance	to illustrate
such as	much like
in the same way as	similar to

5. **Emphasis signals** (This is important):

a major development	it all boils down to
a significant factor	most of all
a primary concern	most noteworthy
a key feature	more than anything else

"The Reading Teacher's Book of Lists, © 1984 Prentice-Hall, Inc., Englewood Cliffs, NJ 07632. By E. Fry, J. Polk, and D. Fountoukidis."

a major event	pay particular attention to
a vital force	remember that
a central issue	should be noted
a distinctive quality	the most substantial issue
above all	the main value
especially important	the basic concept
especially relevant	the crux of the matter
especially valuable	the chief outcome
important to note	the principal item

6. **Cause, condition, or result signals** (Condition or modification coming up):

because	if	of
for	from	so
while	then	but
that	until	since
as	whether	in order that
so that	therefore	unless
yet	thus	due to
resulting from	consequently	

7. **Spatial signals** (Answers the "where" question):

between	on	by
here	there	left
right	these	close to
near	this	side
middle	west	beside
east	about	north
south	around	over
under	away	in front of
across	into	behind
toward	beyond	above
below	opposite	upon
outside	inside	alongside
over	out	far
in	adjacent	near
next to		

8. **Comparison-contrast signals** (We will now compare idea A with idea B):

and	or	also
too	best	most

either	less	less than
more than	same	better
even	then	half
much as	like	analogous to
but	different from	still
yet	however	although
opposite	rather	while
though		

9. **Conclusion signals** (This ends the discussion and may have special importance):

as a result	consequently	finally
from this we see	in conclusion	in summary
hence	last of all	therefore

10. **Fuzz signals** (Idea not exact, or author not positive and wishes to qualify a statement):

almost	if	looks like
maybe	could	some
except	should	alleged
nearly	might	reputed
seems like	was reported	proported
sort of	probably	

11. **Nonword emphasis signals**
exclamation point (!)
<u>underline</u>
italics
bold type
subheads, like <u>The Conclusion</u>
    indention of paragraph
graphic illustrations
numbered points (1, 2, 3)
very short sentence: *Stop war.*
"quotation marks"

Propaganda Techniques—It's Propaganda if It's Used Against You; It's Persuasion if It's Used by You

Name calling—Using a derogatory term to create a negative emotional attitude for an individual or thing. ("You don't want a polluting, gas-guzzling automobile! Buy a milliped cycle instead!"

Glittering generality—Using a shred of truth as a base for a sweeping generalization. ("His past experience as Mar County chairman makes him the best qualified of the three candidates.)

Card stacking—Telling the facts for one side only. "This method of staff reduction cuts operating costs; reduces insurance, pension, and other long-range costs; and provides for easier staff training and supervision." The firing of 60 teachers and doubling of classes is not mentioned.)

Testimonials—Using the testimony of someone to persuade you to think as they do. ("I would never have believed that there was such a difference in hair color products. Then I tried Sizzlelights. My hair never looked so shimmery. For shimmery hair I will always use Sizzlelights.")

Prestige identification—Using a well-known figure to lend importance or prestige to a product. (The TV personality who explains the simple aim-and-shoot procedure for cameras, the benefits of decaffeinated coffee, or the superior quality of a cooking oil.)

Bandwagon—Using the argument that everyone's doing it, so you should, too. ("30 million Americans can't be wrong. They buy B-stone tires at their local B-stone store. Join those who know a value. Buy B-stone!")

Plain folks—Someone just like you, who has your problems and understands your life, uses X product. Therefore, you should, too. (An older, not very attractive woman demonstrates that holding a frypan is painful for her because of arthritis. She then uses X product, there is a time lapse, and she states that the pain is gone, and now she can lift the pan effortlessly. Therefore, if you suffer from painful arthritis as she does, you also will be relieved of the pain by using X.)

Red herring—Highlighting a minor detail as a way to draw attention from the important issue. ("Never-ware cookware will look beautiful on your shelf for generations!" No mention of its cooking value is made.)

Exigency—Creating the impression that your action is required immediately, or the opportunity will be lost forever. ("For a short time only, the limited, signed edition of *Gladstoned* is being offered. Don't wait another minute. Order yours, now, before supplies are depleted.")

Transfer—Attempting to have you transfer your feelings about one thing to another thing. ("Make your home a showplace. Get NU-Color shutters today and be proud of your home.")

Innuendo—Hinting that there may be something being kept hidden. ("Only John T. Belt did not voluntarily disclose his financial position before the primary.")

Snob appeal—Trying to persuade by making you feel you're one of the elite if you use brand X or think Y. ("Live a legend of elegance with Lennet china and crystal. Limited edition available to club members only.")

"The Reading Teacher's Book of Lists, © 1984 Prentice-Hall, Inc., Englewood Cliffs, NJ 07632. By E. Fry, J. Polk, and D. Fountoukidis."

Flag waving—Connecting the use of a product with patriotism. ("Switch to American coal. Let's end our dependency on foreign oil." "Let's make our town (school, company, team, etc.) the best.")

What to Include in Your Study Skills Unit

I. Reading
Using signal words
Using text aids
- Table of Contents
- Introduction
- Headings
- Summaries
- Glossaries
- Appendix
- Index
Surveying the text
Reading to answer questions
Determining organizational patterns
- Chronological
- Cause and effect
- Comparison–contrast
- Functional
- Simple to complex
Pencil activities
- Underlining
- Note taking
- Outlining
- Summarizing
- Graphing
Reading for different purposes
- Skimming
- Scanning
- Reading to learn
- Reading for pleasure
Increasing reading speed

II. Using Visual Aids
Maps (reading and symbols)
Pictures
Graphs (comprehending)
Tables

III. Listening to Lectures
Taking lecture notes
Listening skills

IV. Preparing for Tests
Making study sheets
Making test questions
Recitation or self-testing
Mnemonic techniques
Making a time planning chart

V. Taking a Test
Essay exams
Objective exams
- Multiple choice
- Matching
- True–false

VI. Writing a Research Paper
Using the library
Using reference books
Narrowing a topic
Making a bibliography
Using note cards
Organizing the paper

NEW DEVELOPMENTS AND IDEAS IN READING

Almost every teacher has taken a reading course or two in college. But how do you stay abreast of happenings in the field and get new ideas? The answer is to read the professional journals and to join professional associations that host local and national conferences.

The International Reading Association (IRA) is particularly active and large. It publishes the two most widely circulated reading journals in the world: *The Reading Teacher* for elementary levels, and the *Journal of Reading* for intermediate and secondary levels. It also publishes the *Reading Research Quarterly,* a strictly research-oriented journal. The IRA has an organization in each state and many local chapters.

The National Council of Teachers of English approaches reading as part of language arts. Their journal for elementary teachers is particularly strong in suggesting good books to read and techniques that include writing.

Membership information or journal subscription information can be obtained by writing to any of the organizations.

Other useful addresses are those of publishers of instructional materials. Often, the texts or materials we have on hand have just the publisher's name. If you want to reorder or request catalogues or other information you need their addresses. Here they are.

Five Major Reading Journals

Journal of Reading (general and secondary orientation) International Reading Association. Eight issues yearly.

Journal of Reading Behavior (research orientation) National Reading Conference. Quarterly.

The Reading Teacher (elementary teacher orientation) International Reading Association. Eight issues yearly. (Formerly *Journal of Developmental Reading.*)

Reading Research Quarterly (research orientation) International Reading Association. Quarterly.

Reading World (general and college orientation) College Reading Association. Quarterly.

Language Arts (elementary teacher and language arts orientation) National Council of Teachers of English. Eight issues. (Formerly *Elementary English.*)

Reading Organization Addresses

International Reading Association (IRA)*
Box 8139
Newark, DE 19711
Annual meeting, late April.

National Reading Conference (NRC)
1230 17th Street, N.W.
Washington, DC 20036
Annual meeting, early December.

College Reading Association (CRA)
3340 South Danbury Avenue
Springfield, MO 65807
Annual meeting, October.

National Council of Teachers of English (NCTE)
1111 Kenyon Road
Urbana, IL 81801
Annual meeting, mid-November.

Addresses of Publishers of Curriculum Materials and Tests

Addison-Wesley Publishing Company, Jacob Way, Reading, MA 01867.
Allyn and Bacon, Inc., 470 Atlantic Avenue, Boston, MA 02210.
American Book Company, 135 West 5th Street, New York, NY 10020.
Bantam Books, Inc., 666 Fifth Avenue, New York, NY 10019.
Barnell Loft and Dexter Westbrook Publications, 958 Church Street, Baldwin, NY 11510.
Benefic Press, 1900 North Narragansett, Chicago, IL 60639.
Bobbs-Merrill Company, 4300 West 62nd Street, Indianapolis, IN 46368.
The Center for Applied Research in Education, Inc., P.O. Box 130, West Nyack, NY 10995.
The Continental Press, Inc., 520 East Bainbridge Street, Elizabethtown, PA 17022.
Croft Educational Services, 100 Garfield Avenue, New London, CT 06320.
CTB/McGraw-Hill (California Test Bureau), Del Monte Research Park, Monterey, CA 93940.

---

*Note: Many state and local councils and national affiliates of the International Reading Association hold regular meetings and publish either journals or newsletters on reading. A complete list of them can be obtained without charge from the IRA.

Dreier Educational Systems, *see* Jamestown Publishers.

The Economy Company, P.O. Box 25308, Oklahoma City, OK 73125.

Educational Development Corporation (EDC), P.O. Box 25308, Tulsa, OK 74145.

Educational Development Laboratories (EDL/McGraw-Hill), 1221 Avenue of the Americas, New York, NY 10020.

ERIC/RCS/NCTE, 1111 Kenyon Road, Urbana, IL 61801.

Fearon Publishers, Inc. (Pitman Publishing Corporation), 6 Davis Drive, Belmont, CA 94002.

Follett Publishing Company, 1010 West Washington Boulevard, Chicago, IL 60607.

Garrard Publishing Company, 107 Cherry Street, New Canaan, CT 06840.

Ginn and Company, 191 Spring Street, Lexington, MA 02173.

Globe Book Company, Inc., 175 Fifth Avenue, New York, NY 10010.

Harcourt Brace Jovanovich, Inc., 757 Third Avenue, New York, NY 10017.

Harper and Row, 10 East 53rd Street, New York, NY 10022.

D. C. Heath and Company, 125 Spring Street, Lexington, MA 02173.

Holt, Rinehart and Winston, Inc., 383 Madison Avenue, New York, NY 10017.

Houghton Mifflin Company, 2 Park Street, Boston, MA 02107.

Ideal School Supply Company, 11000 South Lavergne Avenue, Oak Lawn, IL 60453.

Imperial International Learning Corporation, P.O. Box 548, Kankakee, IL 60901.

Instructional Fair, Inc., 4158 Lake Michigan Drive, Grand Rapids, MI 49504.

Instructional Objectives Exchange, 11411 West Jefferson Boulevard, Culver City, CA 90230.

Instructo/McGraw-Hill, Cedar Hollow Road, Paoli, PA 19301.

The Instructor Publications, Inc., 17410 Gilmore Street, Van Nuys, CA 91406.

International Reading Association, 800 Barksdale Road, Newark, DE 19711.

Jamestown Publishers, P.O. Box 6743, Providence, RI 02940.

King Features, 235 East 45th Street, New York, NY 10017.

Laidlaw Brothers, Thatcher and Madison, River Forest, IL 60305.

Learn, Inc., 113 Gaither Drive, Mount Laurel, NJ 08057.

J. B. Lippincott Company, 521 Fifth Avenue, New York, NY 10017.

Lyons and Carnahan, *see* Rand McNally.

Macmillan Publishing Company, Inc., 866 Third Avenue, New York, NY 10022.

McCormick-Mathers Publishing Company (Litton-American Book), 135 West 50th Street, New York, NY 10020.

McGraw-Hill Book Company, 1221 Avenue of the Americas, New York, NY 10020.

Charles E. Merrill Publishing Company, 1300 Alum Creek Drive, Columbus, OH 43216.

Milliken Publishing Company, 1100 Research Boulevard, St. Louis, MO 63132.

Milton Bradley Company, Springfield, MA 01101.

Modern Curriculum Press, Inc., 13900 Prospect Road, Cleveland, OH 44136.

National Council of Teachers of English, 1111 Kenyon Road, Urbana, IL 61801.

New Readers Press, Laubach Literacy, Inc., Box 131, Syracuse, NY 13210.

Open Court Publishing Company, P.O. Box 599, LaSalle, IL 61301.

Parker Publishing Company, Inc., Route 59 at Brookhill Drive, West Nyack, NY 10995.

Prentice-Hall, Inc., Englewood Cliffs, NJ 07632.

The Psychological Corporation, 304 East 45th Street, New York, NY 10017.

Rand McNally and Company, P.O. Box 7600, Chicago, IL 60680.

Random House, Inc., 201 East 50th Street, New York, NY 10022.

Reader's Digest Services, Inc., Pleasantville, NY 10570.

Frank Schaffer Publications, 1926 Pacific Coast Highway, Redondo Beach, CA 90277.

Scholastic Magazines and Book Services, 50 West 44th Street, New York, NY 10036.

Science Research Associates, Inc. (SRA), 155 North Wacker Drive, Chicago, IL 60606.

Scott, Foresman and Company, 1900 East Lake Avenue, Glenview, IL 60025.

Silver Burdett, 250 James Street, Morristown, NJ 07960.

Teachers College Press, 1234 Amsterdam Avenue, New York, NY 10027.

Webster/McGraw-Hill, *see* McGraw-Hill.

Richard L. Zweig Associates, Inc., 20800 Beach Boulevard, P.O. Box 73, Huntington Beach, CA 92648.

SOMETHING TO THINK ABOUT ON A DULL DAY

All books and old ideas make for a very dull day of teaching. Here are a few new ideas for you to bounce off the walls of your teachers' room.

Murphy's Law and other principles might amuse or bemuse. Some have a little jab of truth in them.

The Euphemisms might stand you in good stead at report card time or for parent interviews. They might also take some of the puffery out of some reports you may have to read. Incidentally, your students are no strangers to euphemisms. Have a little lesson with them on euphemisms. Both you and they will have some fun and might learn something new about your language.

The Wacky Words that follow are a rather new twist added by word afficionados. These rebuses represent a familiar phrase, saying, cliché, or name. They're a great pastime for a rainy or snowy afternoon, or as a contest or an introduction to idioms and clichés. Have fun with these. Then have the students create their own.

To add to students' interest in words and language, you also might keep a good assortment of commercial games that students enjoy on the shelves in your classroom. Some favorites are *Scrabble, Boggle, Word Rummy, Spill-and-Spell, Facts-in-Fives,* and *Password.*

Murphy's Law and Other Important Principles

Society is governed by certain immutable laws and principles. Murphy's Law, though of somewhat doubtful authorship, is none the less real. Ask any engineer, mechanic, office manager, or computer programmer.

Both the Peter Principle and Parkinson's Law were developed by very real college professors and both are explained somewhat seriously in full books.

The other principles given here are sometimes original and sometimes borrowed from the common folklore. Use them and amuse with them as needed. Both you and your students might like to add to this important list of real-life observations for fun and profitable insight.

Murphy's Law: If anything can go wrong, it will, and at the worst possible moment.
Peter Principle: In a hierarchy every employee tends to rise to his or her level of incompetence.
Parkinson's Law: Work expands to fill time available for its completion.
Fry's Observation: The more obnoxious the kid, the less he or she will be absent.
Kling's Axiom: Any simple idea can be worded in a complicated way.

No matter how hard you teach a thing, some student is certain not to learn it.

"The Reading Teacher's Book of Lists, © 1984 Prentice-Hall, Inc., Englewood Cliffs, NJ 07632. By E. Fry, J. Polk, and D. Fountoukidis."

Everything takes longer than you think.

The other line always moves faster.

The greater the hurry, the slower the traffic.

No amount of careful planning will ever beat dumb luck.

A good theory might be worth a thousand words, but that won't make it any
    more practical.

School budgets are always cut in a manner so as to create the most disruption.

There are three kinds of lies: white lies, damned lies, and statistics.

A camel is a horse put together by committee.

Extracurricular activities sometimes are neither extra nor curricular.

One person's exuberance is the next person's annoyance.

Principals may come and principals may go, but the secretary will run the
    school regardless.

You can plan anything you like; just don't expect it to happen that way.

Things don't get lost, but they sometimes are carefully put in some strange
    places.

People who ask for just a minute of your time don't have very accurate
    watches.

There's got to be a way to eliminate the last few days of school.

Just when you are sure kids are no good, one of them will do something nice
    for you.

Maybe a school could exist without heat, light, and water, but take away the
    duplicating machine and it would have to close down.

If Saint Peter uses multiple choice tests, we are all in for trouble.

Whoever said the worst students aren't creative? Look at their excuses.

Euphemisms—How to Put It Mildly for the Report Card

Lies	Shows difficulty in distinguishing between imaginary and factual material.
Is a klutz	Has difficulty with motor control and coordination.
Needs nagging	Accomplishes task when interest is constantly prodded.
Fights	Resorts to physical means of winning his or her point or attracting attention.
Smells bad	Needs guidance in development of good habits of hygiene.
Cheats	Needs help in learning to adhere to rules and standards of fair play.
Steals	Needs help in learning to respect the property rights of others.

"The Reading Teacher's Book of Lists, © 1984 Prentice-Hall, Inc., Englewood Cliffs, NJ 07632. By E. Fry, J. Polk, and D. Fountoukidis."

Is a wise guy or gal	Needs guidance in learning to express himself or herself respectfully.
Is lazy	Requires ongoing supervision in order to work well.
Is rude	Lacks a respectful attitude toward others.
Is selfish	Needs help in learning to enjoy sharing with others.
Is gross	Needs guidance in developing the social graces.
Has big mouth	Needs to develop quieter habits of communication.
Eats like a pig	Needs to develop more refined table manners.
Bullies others	Has qualities of leadership but needs to use them more constructively.
Is babyish	Shows lack of maturity in relationships with others.
Hangs out	Seems to feel secure only in group situations; needs to develop sense of identity and independence.
Is disliked by others	Needs help in developing meaningful peer relationships.
Is often late	Needs guidance in developing habits of responsibility and punctuality.
Is truant	Needs to develop a sense of responsibility in regard to attendance.

Wacky Wordies—A Way to Spark Interest in Words

The object in solving is to discern a familiar phrase, saying,
cliché, or name from each arrangement of letters and/or symbols. For example, box 1a depicts the phrase "Eggs over
easy." Box 1b shows "Trafalgar Square." The puzzles get
more diabolical as you go.

	a	b	c	d	e	f
1	eggs easy	T R A F A L G A R	told told tales	e t t r i k c i t p	new leaf	silky
2	price	L +O SS	swear bible bible bible bible	league	bridge water	school
3	–attitude	hoppin	century	E R C O T N U	orseman	D UC K
4	set one's teeth	or or O	bet one's dollar	tpmerhao	what must	way yield
5	t o 2 par n	dictnry	rifle rifle rifle rifle	PAINS	everything pizza	L Y I N G JOB
6	tr ial	prosperity	monkey O	busines	writer's	moon sonata
7	power	mesnackal	Wilson	pit	wheel wheel drive wheel wheel	counter ✓✓✓

black

1a Eggs over easy	2f High school	4e What goes up must come down	6b Prosperity is just around the corner
1b Trafalgar Square	3a Negative attitude	4f Yield right of way	6c Monkey around
1c Twice-Told Tales	3b Shopping center	5a Not up to par	6d Unfinished business
1d Round-trip ticket	3c Turn-of-the-century	5b Abridged dictionary	6e Writer's cramp
1e Turn over a new leaf	3d Counterclockwise	5c Repeating rifle	6f Moonlight Sonata
1f Pie in the sky	3e Headless Horseman	5d Growing pains	7a Power blackout
2a The Price Is Right	3f Sitting duck	5e Pizza with everything on it	7b Between-meal snack
2b Total loss	4a Set one's teeth on edge	5f Lying down on the job	7c Flip Wilson
2c Swear on a stack of Bibles	4b Double or nothing	6a Trial separation	7d Bottomless pit
2d Little League	4c Bet one's bottom dollar		7e Four-wheel drive
2e Bridge over troubled water	4d Mixed metaphor		7f Checkout counter

Reprinted from *Games* Magazine (515 Madison Avenue, New York NY 10022). Copyright© 1980
Playboy Enterprises, Inc.

The object in solving is to discern a familiar phrase, saying, cliché, or name from each arrangement of letters and/or symbols. For example, box 1a depicts "once over lightly." Box 1b shows "gossip column." Sounds easy, but wait until you see the others.

	a	b	c	d	e	f
1	once lightly	g o s s i p	wave radio	c a p n t a i	noon good	bathing suit
2	ee ch sp	God nation ✳	✓ yearly	ses ame	d deer e r	hold second
3	r−i×s+k	pox	strokes *strokes* **strokes**	n P y o c m a	law of reтurns	e a p s u a l
4	hou se	age beauty	harm on y	encounters encounters encounters	breth	hearted
5	p a r t i c i p l e	MAN campus	momanon	⌐ld block	"Duty!" and beyond	day day
6	sigh	qonpʃ	skating ice	inflat10n	g o s p e l	enemy enemy
7	to ngue ngue	gettingitall	e a v e s	c m r e a ban ana	e e q u a l s m c	aluminum

Names of contributors appear in parentheses following their answers:

1a Once over lightly (Karen Sayer, Ann Arbor, MI)
1b Gossip column (E. J. Ridler, Depew, NY)
1c Short-wave radio (Mary Sampley, St. Petersburg, FL)
1d Captain Hook (Karen Sayer, Ann Arbor, MI)
1e Good afternoon (Jim Tarolli, Rocky River, OH)
1f Topless bathing suit (Gifted class of Matteson School District 162, Matteson, IL)
2a Parts of speech (Ann Madura, Yonkers, NY)
2b One nation, under god, indivisible (Jamie Lubin, Randolph, NJ)
2c Yearly checkup (Richard Janssen, Churchville, PA)
2d Open sesame (David Reifer, Garden Grove, CA)
2e Deer crossing (Jamie Lubin, Randolph, NJ)
2f Hold on a second (The Imberts, Belcourt, ND)
3a Calculated risk (Barbara DePaoli, Brockton, MA)
3b Smallpox (Stephen Sundel, South Orange, NJ)
3c Different strokes (E. J. Ridler, Depew, NY)
3d Mixed company (Bradley W. Brunsell, Milton, MA)
3e Law of diminishing returns (Karen Sayer, Ann Arbor, MI)
3f Round of applause (Said Zeiba, Bellevue, WA)
4a Split-level house (Karen Sayer, Ann Arbor, MI)
4b Age before beauty (Colleen Brady, Malverne, NY)
4c Three-part harmony (Karen Sayer, Ann Arbor, MI)
4d Close Encounters of the Third Kind (Jamie Lubin, Randolph, NJ)
4e A little out of breath (Bradley W. Brunsell, Milton, MA)
4f Light-hearted (Ann Madura, Yonkers, NY)

5a Dangling participle (Karen Sayer, Ann Arbor, MI)
5b Big man on campus (Josh Tarnow, South Orange, NJ)
5c Man in the moon (Bradley W. Brunsell, Milton, MA)
5d Chip off the old block (Jim Galvez, Santa Maria, CA)
5e Above and beyond the call of duty (Rob McDonough, Hamilton, OH)
5f Day in and day out (Beth Eason, Atherton, CA)
6a No end in sight (Barbara DePaoli, Brockton, MA)
6b Shadow of a doubt (Karen Sayer, Ann Arbor, MI)
6c Skating on thin ice (Ann Madura, Yonkers, NY)
6d Double-digit inflation (Vicki Sheskin, Bethel, CT)
6e Spread the gospel (Virginia McLaughlin, Sherman Oaks, CA)
6f Archenemies (Karen Sayer, Ann Arbor, MI)
7a Forked tongue (Howie Orona, Grand Valley, CO)
7b Getting it all together (David Reifer, Garden Grove, CA)
7c Eavesdropping (Leonard M. Levine, New York, NY)
7d Banana split with whipped cream topping (Leonard M. Levine, New York, NY)
7e $E = mc^2$ (Danny McClelland, Carmichael, CA)
7f Aluminum siding (Evanne & Peter Kofman, Phoenix, AZ)

In cases where the same rebus was contributed by more than one person, we chose the entry with the earlier postmark.

If you enjoyed "Yet Wackier Wordies," we recommend the new Bantam book WORDoodles by Marvin Miller (paperback, $1.25).